Advance Praise for

JOURNALING BY THE MOONLIGHT
A Mother's Path to Self-Discovery

☾

"Motherhood is a challenging journey and women often lose themselves in the overwhelm of the job, despite its joyful moments and precious expressions of love. With this book, Tina offers a cornucopia of hope to women who find themselves spinning in circles in the dark, caught in the terror of being true to themselves while simultaneously trying to take exquisite care of their little ones. Tina shares her personal story of healing and how journaling guided her to the truth about her angst as a mother, allowed her to reclaim her inner wisdom, and ultimately reconnect with her soul. This journey to center led Tina to her life purpose of supporting mothers by lighting a passage out of the darkness for them to follow and become whole and fulfilled. Using the moon as a potent metaphor, Tina sparks self-awareness with her journaling prompts and creative exercises that guide mothers into becoming empowered and serene. Read this book and claim your entwined roles as woman and mother, and then give this book to every woman you know who needs to awaken to her own essential self-expression. Tina embodies the courage to lead today's mothers into a community with each other, enabling them to raise the next generation of healthy and well-adjusted boys and girls, while living a full life themselves".

~ *Gail McMeekin, LICSW, author of The 12 Secrets of Highly Creative Women: A Portable Mentor, www.creativesuccess.com*

✶ ✶ ✶ ✶ ✶ ✶ ✶ ✶

"Tina M. Games brings to light the conflicts of motherhood which most of us mothers feel – yet may not feel comfortable divulging or/and exploring. With compassion and by telling her own story, she takes you by the hand and walks you through a process of moonlit journaling – a process which every mother would benefit!"

~ *Ruth Folit, director of the International Association for Journal Writing and creator of Life Journal Software, www.iajw.org*

✶ ✶ ✶ ✶ ✶ ✶ ✶ ✶

"When I was a young mother in search of myself, I'd gaze at the moon for inspiration. I would have welcomed Tina Games' wise and gentle guide on my search for an authentic self. Tina's journaling method is a gift of wisdom that will shine a light on your inner journey. As a grandmother now, I'm inspired to use her prompts to reconnect with the moon and its phases to enhance my creative reflections. This book has wonderful wisdom for women of any age."

~ Linda Joy Myers, Ph.D., author of The Power of Memoir – How to Write Your Healing Story, and president of the National Association of Memoir Writers, www.namw.org

* * * * * * * *

"A 'must read' for every mother, *Journaling By The Moonlight* is a wonderful resource to empower women to tap into their authentic self and live their life to the fullest, casting aside all 'rules' about who a mother should or shouldn't be. The journaling exercises provide for a wonderful path of self discovery to enable us to become better mothers, wives, daughters, grandmothers, but above all else, women who are not defined by our roles, but instead by who we truly are. As Tina so profoundly says, Motherhood may only be part of our purpose – and that is okay. When we follow our heart and discover our own personal path, we find true happiness, set a great example for our children and become a shining light in the world."

~ Debbie LaChusa, founder of the National Association of Home-Based Business Moms and Author of The Career-at-Home Mom, www.nahbm.com

* * * * * * * *

"This book is a gem and a MUST for every mother who wants to deepen the process of motherhood as well as cultivate or enhance her creative prowess and connection to herself. Using the magnetism of the moon, Tina is the Muse of Journaling Moms. She has made this book enchanting, irresistible, and inviting for moms to reflect on a time of life they want to savor and survive."

~ Jill Badonsky, author of The Awe-manac: A Daily Dose of Wonder and The Nine Modern Day Muses (and a Bodyguard), www.themuseisin.com

* * * * * * * *

"*Journaling by the Moonlight* has such a powerful purpose in the world. Tina's support, inspiration, and insight not only allow mothers to explore themselves and become more of who they were meant to be, Tina is also empowering generations to come – spiritually healthy moms create healthy children and healthy communities. As Tina shows mothers how to heal through journaling, she is literally healing the world."

~ Sheri McConnell, Founder and President of the National Association of Women Writers, www.naww.org

* * * * * * * *

"Tina Games has done something extraordinary with this book! – She is a moonbeam of light that brings support, compassion and strength. Tina illuminates the path for any mother to gain access and redefine her authentic inner self."

~ Beverly Down, Creative Life Coach, StarCreativityCoaching.com

* * * * * * * *

Journaling by the Moonlight

A Mother's Path to Self-Discovery

☾

Tina M. Games
Creativity and Life Purpose Coach

Moonlight Muse Press

Journaling by the Moonlight
A Mother's Path to Self-Discovery
Tina M. Games

Photo images created by Lani Phillips, Wise Women Ink

Illustrations (p.139-140) by Laura Wallace, Worx Graphic Design

ISBN: 978-1-936214-04-4
Library of Congress Control Number: 2010921416

Copyright ©2010 by Tina M. Games

All rights reserved. No part of this book may be used or reproduced in any manner whatsoever without written permission of the editor/copyright owner except in the case of brief quotations embodied in articles or reviews.

Book design by Nancy Cleary, Wyatt-MacKenzie

Published by Moonlight Muse Press
An Imprint of Wyatt-MacKenzie

www.wyattmackenzie.com

JOURNALING BY THE MOONLIGHT
A Mother's Path to Self-Discovery

☾

Dedication

This book is dedicated to my mother, who sacrificed quite a bit of herself to be a mother to four children. Her strength and perseverance through times of turmoil – and without the help of a strong support system – gave me the inspiration to be a bigger voice for mothers who feel like they have lost their way.

Table of Contents

☾

ACKNOWLEDGMENTS	xi
FOREWORD – by Kathleen Adams, LPC, PTR	xiii
CHAPTER ONE – By the Light of the Moon	15
CHAPTER TWO – Starting our Journey with the Moon: Dedicating your Journal	21
CHAPTER THREE – Dancing on Moonbeams – The Power of Journal Writing	25
CHAPTER FOUR – Cultural and Religious Awareness and the Symbolism of the Moon	32
CHAPTER FIVE – The Power of the Moon: Astrological Influences in Spiritual Transformation	40
CHAPTER SIX – The New Moon: The Beginning of a Quest for Self-Discovery	47
CHAPTER SEVEN – The Waxing Crescent: Who Are You, Really?	53
CHAPTER EIGHT – The First Quarter: Dealing With Mother's Guilt and Resentment	65
CHAPTER NINE – The Waxing Gibbous: The Strength of a Support System	73
CHAPTER TEN – The Full Moon: Identifying Your True Self	87
CHAPTER ELEVEN – The Waning Gibbous: Creating the Bigger Picture	97
CHAPTER TWELVE – The Last Quarter: Taking Baby Steps	105
CHAPTER THIRTEEN – The Waning Crescent: Managing the Ebb and Flow	115
CHAPTER FOURTEEN – The Blue Moon: Celebrating Your Uniqueness	123
CHAPTER FIFTEEN – Looking in the Mirror and Dancing by Moonlight	131
CHAPTER SIXTEEN – Resources for the Journaling Mom	139
ABOUT THE AUTHOR	145

JOURNALING BY THE MOONLIGHT
A Mother's Path to Self-Discovery

☾

Acknowledgments

Writing this book has truly been a journey. I've met some wonderful people along the way – all of whom were willing to share their wisdom in helping me craft this project.

I want to thank my mother, first and foremost, for being who she is – and for showing me that it's okay to feel the way you feel and to know that everything happens for a reason. It's what led me to create this self-discovery process and to put it in book form.

And I want to thank the many mothers who opened up to me – and shared their stories. There's tremendous value when women come together and embrace each other unconditionally. When truth is told, personal growth can begin.

A special thanks goes to Kathleen (Kay) Adams who served as my mentor in connecting personal writing with personal growth. Kay is a pioneer in the field of journal therapy and believes strongly in the power of journal writing as a form of personal healing.

I'd like to also thank my writing coach, Suzanne Lieurance for guiding me on the process of putting this book together – and my business coach, Sheri McConnell for convincing me that this book could change lives. It has always been my mission to pull mothers out of their darkness and reconnect them with their light – and Suzanne and Sheri fully understood the journey I was on and supported me every step of the way.

Thanks also go to Nancy Cleary, my book publisher – and to Lani Phillips of Wise Women Ink, who served as a consultant for the creation and publication of the accompanying deck of journaling cards. Both of these amazingly talented women immediately connected to my bigger vision and wholeheartedly agreed to be a part of the journey.

I'd also like to thank the many women in my personal and business circles who watched this book go from an idea to something they could hold in their hands. And in particular, I'd like to thank members of the Alexandria Commission for Women who saw the value in creating support systems for mothers so they could live life with zest and be fully present for their children.

And my biggest thanks of all is reserved for my family – my husband Simon, and my two children, Spencer and Holly, who lived through the mommy experience with me. They rode the waves of emotion as I charted my way through the motherhood course – and became a better person and a better mother every step of the way. I wouldn't be where I am now with you!

And to every mother who reads this book, I hope that you will be forever changed as you step into your own light and into your own power. As mothers, we have the ability to change the world through the seeds we sow. But the seeds can't be planted without attention to our own self-care and to our own self-love. I thank you for having the courage to face your own truth – and for having belief in your own self-worth. It's YOU who makes this journey worthwhile!

Journaling by the Moonlight
A Mother's Path to Self-Discovery

Foreword

By Kathleen Adams, LPC, PTR
Founder/Director, The Center for Journal Therapy

* * * * * * * *

At the heart and soul of nearly every book on contemporary journal writing, you'll find two things: The author's desire to help others gain insight, clarity and peace of mind through writing, and the weaving of the author's own story of how writing transformed struggle into strength.

This remarkable book is no exception. Tina Games offers her considerable knowledge and expertise as a life coach who facilitates others along the path to self-discovery. She shares her own story of soul-wrenching conflict after her children were born, trapped among the layers of her maternal love, depression over her loss of sense of self, pervasive guilt and ensuing grief. Tina's story of writing by the moonlight, when stark darkness and quiet descended, is both metaphorically and pragmatically powerful. Guided by the moon's symbols and rhythms, she found her own path in the pages of her journal. She emerged empowered and balanced.

It is that voice of clarity, strength and encouragement that rings out on every page, in every Moonlight Musing, in every fascinating tidbit of moon lore. Tina Games invites you, the reader, on a moonlit voyage that she herself has traveled. Her compass is the time-tested wisdom of journal techniques and processes that she has practiced for years.

I first met Tina when her children, Spencer and Holly, were toddlers. She came to me with the email moniker of "JournalingMom" and a thirst to bring this transformational work to others.

After completing the distance-learning *Journal to the Self*® Instructor Certification Training, Tina launched into teaching with such exuberance and gusto that I knew there were great things ahead.

And great things there have been. Tina's focus on "moonlight moms" has become a niche that stretches out across the life span. From her starting point of young mothers, she has expanded her work into mothers of adolescents, empty-nesting mothers, grandmothers, daughters who care for aging mothers, stepmothers, foster mothers, adoptive mothers. If there is a real or symbolic umbilical bond, Tina brings her wisdom, compassion and expertise.

It was 1985 when I birthed the work that has become known as *Journal to the Self*, and like any mid-life mother, I am proud and gratified that my first-born has grown into a mature, capable adult that does good work in the world. Among my greatest prides over the past quarter-century are the many outstanding individuals I've mentored who are becoming the next voices of therapeutic writing. Tina Games, through her devotion not only to her own family but to her own authentic self, has entered into her own fullness and now shines a pathway of light for others to follow. You're in good hands. May your own moonlight musings be blessed.

Kathleen Adams, LPC, PTR
Director, Center for Journal Therapy
Denver, Colorado
Full Moon, November 2009

Chapter One
By the Light of the Moon

*The purpose of life is to live it, to taste experience to the utmost,
to reach out eagerly and without fear for newer and richer experience.*
~ Eleanor Roosevelt

☾

My Relationship with the Moon

I've always had a fascination with the moon. After studying the phases of the moon in astronomy classes and the astrological impact it can have on personal transformation, I began to explore the spiritual connections that the moon has brought to many cultures over thousands of years. No matter where we are in the world, we can see the moon. It's something that we all have in common.

The moon has brought great comfort to me in my life, particularly during a time when I I felt a loss of personal identity. This was during my first two years of becoming a mother – a time of joy, but a time of anxiety, depression and confusion. I was a mother, but who was I really? I took many walks during those two years, gazing at the moon and trying to make sense of who I was and what purpose my life served. It was during this journey of self-discovery, that I rediscovered the sense of peace I felt whenever I spent time reflecting by the moonlight.

Taking the knowledge I had of the moon and its place in spiritual transformation, I combined it with my training as a life purpose coach and a journaling workshop facilitator. Together, this combination created a path of self-discovery for me – a path that I want to share with the many mothers who are faced with a major life transition or who feel a loss of personal identity.

My Transition into Motherhood

I'm a mother to two beautiful and loving children – Spencer and Holly. I've learned a lot about myself just by being their mother. They've taught me to stop and smell the roses – literally. Seeing the world through their eyes has been an incredible gift.

They have also taught me the importance of following my heart. What better lesson can we teach our children?

The first and best piece of advice on motherhood I ever received was from my OB/GYN after the birth of my first child, Spencer. During my six-week check-up, my doctor's last words to me before I left her office were, "Remember, if Mama ain't happy, nobody's happy."

She and I had been discussing my desire to return to work. I felt a tremendous amount of guilt over the thought of doing such a thing. Being a stay-at-home Mom seemed to be the "in" thing when my son was a baby, not to mention the choice of so many mothers living in generations before us. My own mother-in-law even commented, "Why have a baby if you're going to have someone else raise him?" And this was followed by our pediatrician asking me, "Do you really have to work? The best thing for a child under two is to be at home with their mother."

It seemed all the odds were against me. Then my OB/GYN saved the day. She convinced me that the best thing for any child is a happy mother. According to her, it didn't matter if the mother wanted to work or she wanted to stay at home with her kids full time. The most important thing was that it had to be the mother's choice.

I attempted to follow my doctor's advice by going back to work. It was something that I wanted to do for myself. Unfortunately, my return to work didn't last long.

My son became vulnerable to what many would call normal childhood illnesses – colds and ear infections. He spent the first nine months of his life in and out of his pediatrician's office, not to mention two overnight stays in the hospital emergency room. It was the outpatient surgery, to put tubes in his ears, that really put me over the edge.

I was consumed with guilt. I felt horribly selfish in my desire to return to a successful career, earning a paycheck that my husband and I knew we could live without.

I did what many mothers would have done. I gave up my career to stay at home with my son. It worked out fine for the first few months. Then it hit me. As much as I adored my child and loved being his mother, my personal identity was gone. I was a mother, but who was I really? Motherhood can be the most rewarding job in the world, but it can also be the most challenging. Like many mothers, I've experienced the incredible joys that my children bring me every day. Unfortunately, I've also experienced the downside of motherhood – depression, anxiety, isolation and low self-esteem.

I was fortunate, however, to have met many mothers on my own journey who were traveling on the same path. I quickly began to realize the strength of a support system with those who could truly empathize with what I was going through.

Mothers are at the core of their children's lives. We have to be strong for them. We all face challenges during our journeys as mothers, some a little more difficult than others. But we're expected to be that rock when our children need us.

The Journey of Motherhood

During the course of my personal journey and the years I've spent as a life coach for mothers who are challenged with the loss of personal identity, I've encountered the many expectations that are placed upon mothers. These are sometimes so heavy, that a mother feels guilty when trying to do anything that doesn't involve her children.

Society puts a lot of pressure on a woman to do what's right for the family. This pressure often comes from well-intentioned individuals who don't fully understand that in order for a mother to be at her best, she needs to fulfill her own needs and desires. And the best way to do this is to live with authenticity.

Martina, a mother of two teenage boys, remembered the criticism she received from her mother-in-law when she opted to take a job offered to her by her previous employer. "My old boss and I had stayed in touch for years. She told me, whenever I was ready, she would have a job waiting for me. Well, after 15 years of being a full-time mother, I was ready to spread my wings and take on a new opportunity. But my mother-in-law had trouble accepting this. She kept reminding me of all the field trips and classroom projects that I'd be missing. When I told her that the boys were perfectly fine with my decision, she just couldn't believe it. 'Motherhood should always be a woman's first priority,' she said to me."

Stereotypes are a hard thing for many to overcome. We often get strong messages that to focus on our own needs is selfish and unfeminine – which is why many women don't focus on their own needs until the end of the day when everyone else is taken care of.

In today's society, it is important for mothers to negotiate to have their needs taken seriously. And part of this negotiation involves letting go of old models and stereotypes.

Having Our Own Identity

Through my own personal research and my work as a life coach, I've had countless conversations with mothers all over the United States and various parts of the world and the message I've gathered is consistent. Women must remember that aside from our roles as mothers, we are individuals with interests and passions. We must be able to fulfill those needs in order to be the best mothers we can be.

It's been this philosophy that has changed the way I live my life and it's helped me to be the best role model I can be for my kids.

So after years of being a mother to two beautiful children and hearing confirmation after confirmation from other mothers in similar situations, I can attest to the pithy advice of my OB/GYN.

This book reveals stories of mothers who have ridden against the current and managed to stay afloat. Designed as a self-discovery journal, it allows for personal reflection that ties into the transformational phases of the moon, with many opportunities to answer the question, "I'm a mother, but who am I really?"

Through the stories and the various creative writing exercises scattered throughout the book, you'll gain a better understanding of who you are and what keeps your passions and desires burning.

Here's to a journey filled with self-discovery and fulfillment!

Moonlight Musings

Think about where you are – right now. What is motherhood like for you? What do you enjoy most about it? What do you find most challenging? Take a few minutes to answer these questions on this page.

Now, setting motherhood aside for a moment and looking at your life as a whole – do you feel fulfilled? If not, think about the areas of your life where you're feeling a void and make a few notes here. We'll be writing about them in more detail in a later chapter.

Chapter Two
Starting our Journey with the Moon
Dedicating Your Journal to Your Spiritual Awakening

Happiness cannot be traveled to, owned, earned, worn or consumed. Happiness is the spiritual experience of living every minute with love, grace and gratitude.
~ Denis Waitley

☾

The Spiritual Awakening

As with any self-discovery process, you're going to stumble across little gems of insight. With this book, in particular, you'll find yourself slowly walking through sparkles of light coming from the moonbeams of wisdom that will be dancing around you.

Be open to whatever comes your way. Allow your inner compass to guide you in the direction that feels most right to you. Words and images will came to you as you dance toward a spiritual awakening – a moment when the energies of the universe pull together to light the path toward living a more authentic life.

This process is very different for each person, so just focus on yourself and your deepest desires. Be totally honest with who you are in this moment – and where you want to go from here. The truth will set you free!

Working with the Moonlight Musings

As you work your way through this book and through the various moon phases, you'll see many highlighted boxes titled, "Moonlight Musing." These are journaling prompts and creative exercises designed to help you better connect with your authentic self – that unique being living inside of you who may be feeling a little trapped at the moment.

Let's open the door for her – allowing her to take small, gentle steps out – and give her the space she needs to pour all of her inner wisdom out onto the pages of your journal. You'll soon find that this person, in all her wisdom, is you – feeling more alive and more connected than ever!

Selecting Your Writing Instrument

Carefully select your writing instrument as you begin on this wonderful journey with your authentic self – underneath the moonlit sky. You'll want to record all of the amazing discoveries that you'll make along the way.

As you select your pen, give careful thought to what feels right in your hand. As the energy moves from your inner being through your mind, your thoughts will begin to flow through your arm to your hand. And you'll feel as if you're channeling your authentic self.

Consider giving her some color, whether it's the color of the ink or simply the color of your pen. Allow her energy to pour through you and onto the page. Pick a writing instrument that represents the energy you're feeling in the moment.

You may find yourself switching pens throughout this process, and that's okay. Go with what feels right for you in the moment – as this will lead you closer to the messages that your authentic self wants you to hear.

Dedicating Your Journal

With any journal that you keep, I highly recommend dedicating it to the intention that you've set for yourself in that particular moment.

In this book, we will be working toward a spiritual connection with your authentic self – one that leads you toward a life filled with purpose, passion and creative expression. As we work through the chapters, we will hold this intention as we weave our way on a path of self-discovery – that begins in darkness, but ends in an amazingly unique shade of light. This will be your light – unique to you and only you.

Moonlight Musings

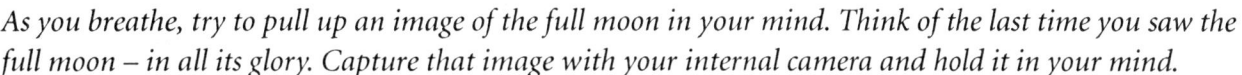

Before we begin on this moonlit path to self-discovery, I'd like to invite you to take a few minutes to sit comfortably with your eyes closed.

Breathe in deeply – and exhale slowly.

Do this several times.

As you breathe, try to pull up an image of the full moon in your mind. Think of the last time you saw the full moon – in all its glory. Capture that image with your internal camera and hold it in your mind.

Think about the wholeness of the full moon. Think about the brightness of the full moon.

And imagine yourself as a whole being – filled with brightness – and filled with purpose. Think of yourself as a being that has the capability to light up the darkness of the night sky.

Hold this image for a few minutes – and breathe deeply – and exhale slowly.

When you're ready, open your eyes and pick up your pen. Open it to this page and write a dedication to yourself – one that represents your desired outcome as we work through this journaling process.

For example, "I dedicate this journal to the discovery of my inner being – who is yearning to connect with a bigger purpose – one that is filled with light and love and laughter. And may the light of the moon guide me on this journey of self-discovery."

Holding the image of the full moon in your mind – and knowing your reasons for embarking on this journey of self-discovery, create a dedication that encapsulates your desire in this very moment.

Make sure to end the dedication with today's date.

And – with all the writing that you will do throughout the chapters in this book, please remember to date everything. This will become important as you continue to travel on this path – to see where you began and to appreciate how far you've come.

Now let's begin.

Chapter Three
Dancing on Moonbeams:
The Power of Journal Writing

Journal writing is a voyage to the interior.
~ Christina Baldwin

☾

During those first two years of motherhood, my journal became my confidante. It was the only place where I could air out all the mixed-up feelings that were swirling around inside of me. And it was a safe place for me to be honest, without fear of judgment.

I found myself writing during my son's nap times – and at night after everyone was in bed. I would curl up in my favorite arm chair, where I could get a glimpse of the moon. And I would enter into a mindset where I felt free of the darkness that seemed to have a hold on me at the time.

The words would just pour out onto the page – and I would cry, mostly out of frustration. I didn't want to feel the way I was feeling. I was so desperate to be free of the thoughts that cluttered my mind. I felt trapped and confused. And I felt like my life was not mine to live the way I wanted. I lived it for my son, my husband – and the others who felt the need to tell me how to be a good mother.

My journal absorbed my every word and eventually gave me the clarity to see that only I had the power to change my course. It led me out of the darkness of the moon – and into the light of the full moon. And I soon began to realize that I could be a much better mother if I was a happier person. Journal writing had freed me from the chains of my emotional pain.

What is Journal Writing?

A journal (or a diary) is a place to record everyday happenings and/or thoughts and feelings. It can be a tool for self-discovery, a place to brainstorm ideas, a safe space to release emotions or an aid to help you sort through feelings of overwhelm and frustration.

Journal writing can also be a tool for spiritual growth. As the words pour out onto the paper, it can reveal inner guidance that can help you make sense out of various scenarios and give some order to your life. It can provide awareness of patterns and offer perspective on the decisions that lie ahead. It can also help clarify beliefs and provide a safe place for self-expression.

Journal writing is a form of therapeutic writing. It's the process of chronicling those many thoughts that are swirling around in your head – with no worries of being censored. During times of deliberation or when you're facing a creative block, journal writing can help. It can be a powerful way to connect with your authentic self and your core beliefs. It can also help you see the many options that will lead you to a bigger vision.

Through your journal, you can process your thoughts and hear the advice and encouragement of your wisest, most loving self. The act of writing things down makes thinking much clearer. It's like taking all of the rambling thoughts out of the mental file and dumping them onto the page to sort out – line by line.

Writing slows down your thoughts and allows you to think more clearly and to process with more clarity. And by writing in your journal, it can help you focus your mind with laser-like accuracy. Slowing down your mind through writing enables you to clearly hear the voice of your soul.

Different Types of Journal Writing

Writing in a journal is a highly individualized experience. There is no "right" way to do it. Whatever works best for you is the ideal. Some people write first thing in the morning while others write at night. And some write in scattered bits throughout the day. Whatever you choose, try to make it consistent if you can – and pick a quiet spot where you won't be interrupted. This will allow the creative juices to flow, making it a comfortable part of your daily routine.

There are many different types of journal writing:

- *Dream journals* allow you to capture the intuitive insights that come to you in dreams.

- *Personal journals* provide you with the space to record your innermost thoughts as they come to you throughout the day.

- *Project journals* enable you to log your progress on a particular long-term endeavor, like writing a book or starting a business.

- *Idea journals* are a perfect container for the creative person who is rich with ideas about potential projects that could evolve in the future.

- *Synchronicity journals* are places where you can log the magical experiences that feel important in the moment and that may prove valuable in the bigger scheme of things.

- *Relationship journals* are special journals where two people can communicate with each other through the written word when speaking may be difficult.

- *Nature journals* can hold observations of outdoor experiences and how they relate to our inner growth.

- *Spiritual journals* provide the journal writer the freedom to record the entire spiritual growth process from beginning to end.

- *Transition journals* are places where one can note every step of a major life transition and how it transforms to the next phase in life's journey.

- *Family journals* are special books where personal notes about a family's history can be recorded and preserved for future generations.

- *Gratitude journals* allow you to capture all that you're grateful for in any given day and support a positive mindset – seeing things from a glass half full versus a glass half empty.

These are just a few types of journals that one can keep. And it's quite possible that a person could keep several different journals at one time, depending on the purpose of each individual journal.

The Benefits of Journal Writing

It has been proven that the act of writing is an aid to emotional release. Much like a therapist, the journal becomes a confidant and a safe place to share your innermost thoughts without worrying about repercussions.

And by releasing unwanted emotions and thoughts, you begin to free your body of tension and stress – which leads to better health overall. It gives you the power to sleep better, to make healthier eating choices and to enjoy life more fully.

Keeping unwanted thoughts and emotions serves no one. All it does is manifest into one big snowball of frustration, resentment, anger – and eventually, depression.

So take a deep breath – and release – and begin to feel your thoughts itching to get out.

Moonlight Musings

Let's do a "mind dump" – which is a clearing of all the mental clutter in your mind.

Whatever you're thinking right now, just dump it out onto the page. Don't worry about making sense. Just dump it all out. Much like a good spring cleaning, go through those closets of your mind and dump out every thought you're having right now.

Then sit with your jumbled thoughts for a few minutes. Read over them a couple of times.

Moonlight Musings

What jumped out at you as you read your thoughts from the previous page? Ponder it for a moment. You may want to highlight or underline anything that feels significant.

Now go back to your notes from the opening chapter. What is motherhood like for you? What do you enjoy most about it? What do you find most challenging? Take a few minutes to record your thoughts on these pages.

Now take a look at your life as a whole. Do you feel fulfilled? If not, think about the areas of your life where you're feeling a void and describe what that feels like.

Continue to write until you have dumped all of these thoughts into this journal.

When you're done, take a deep breath and exhale slowly.

We're about to go dancing on moonbeams!

Chapter Four
Cultural Awareness and the Symbolism of the Moon

"Four nights will quickly dream away the time;
And then the moon, like to a silver bow.
New-bent in heaven, shall behold the night. Of our solemnities."
~ **William Shakespeare, A Midsummer's Night Dream**

☽

The Rhythm of the Moon Cycles

Since our earliest times, our ancestors have recognized that the moon has the power to move the great waters of the world's oceans, giving her a profound influence on the lives of all things that live on this planet.

More and more people are becoming increasingly aware of the fact that the ever-changing rhythms of the moon affect our moods and emotions, our deepest impulses, and our actions and behavior. As she passes through her different phases, the moon's rhythmic movement creates a dynamic energy that washes through us like the coming and going of the tides. How we behave and how we respond to the many things that happen around us every day springs from our personal interaction with the lunar cycles.

Learning to tap into this tempo and to work with the rhythm means that we can capitalize on the energy of the moment. Rather than fighting against the moon cycle, we can move with it – flowing in harmony – which can ride us up to the shore. Falling out of step with these natural rhythms can all too often result in frustration, depression and isolation as we waste a large amount of time and energy struggling against the tide.

The Moon as a Source of Inspiration

Moon teachings are fluid. They wax (grow) and wane (diminish) in relation to the movement of the moon's 28-day cycle. In astrology, the moon under which you were born is called your natal moon and can reflect certain tendencies that are part of your personality. It will also give you guidance as to what your inner strengths are and what your potential weaknesses are.

There was a period in our world's history when people could calculate the time with a quick glance at the moon – where she was in the sky and by the cyclical pattern of her changing shape. The moon's changing face follows a precise pattern that repeats itself every month.

The moon has fascinated and inspired artists, lovers and travelers. Serene and romantic, she lights up the dark midnight skies and transforms everything with her silvery beams of light. Many songs have been written about the moon and it has been the inspiration for many works of art, both visual and literary.

Moonlight Musings

Take a step outside on a clear evening and take in the light of the moon. Sit with the energy for a few minutes, breathing deeply and exhaling slowly.

Now close your eyes and imagine yourself gliding with the energy of the moonbeams. What does this feel like? What is coming to mind?

Take some time to write about this here.

Cultural Associations with the Moon

Many ancient cultures marked time by the lunar cycle. The phases of the moon provided a consistent and easily observable means of counting time. In fact, all calendar months are loosely based on the phases of the Moon.

Since the early times, people have used the movement of the stars and planets – and especially the movement of the Moon with its precise sequences – as a great cosmic clock. It marks the division of day and night. Then blocks of seven days, counted from one lunar phase to the next, create a week. One entire cycle of the moon marks a month.

All calendar months are loosely based on the phases of the Moon. Throughout history, some civilizations have based their calendars purely on the movements of the Moon. Eastern calendars, such as those traditionally used by the Chinese, are based on the movements of the Moon, as is the Islamic month.

In Western calendars, we see a mixture of solar and lunar influences. While Christmas Day is fixed according to the solar time, other holidays such as Easter follow a lunar schedule which is why it always falls on a different day each year. Lunar schedules follow the movement of the moon, which can vary from month to month. This is why the various moon phases begin and end on different days every month.

It's been said that the moon phases influence certain activity on the Earth. For example, law enforcement agencies have reported increases in violent crime around the time of the Full Moon. This typically marks a time of high intensity, so knowing this can create an individual awareness that calls for more patience and understanding – rather than an immediate need to react.

The Hindu Tradition

The Hindu calendar is lunar-based. Because the Indian astrological tradition is a little different from the western tradition, you may find the dates will vary slightly. They use a sidereal system based on where the constellations actually sit in the heavens. But they have the origins of Blue Moon celebrations in their culture going back a thousand years.

The importance of the color blue was derived from the skin color of Lord Krishna, who is revered as the divine flute player. The special energy of the second Moon was considered "blue" or divine by Indian religious scholars and priests. Thus they celebrate two Full Moons in the one sign and had large religious and sacrificial ceremonies to acknowledge the importance of the second.

Native American Spirituality

The Medicine Wheel is representative of Native American Indian spirituality. It symbolizes the individual journey we must each take to find our own path. Within the Medicine Wheel are the four cardinal directions and the four sacred colors. The circle of the wheel represents the Circle of Life and the center of the circle represents the Eternal Fire.

There are other teachings of the Medicine Wheel that are tied to the moon and the lunar cycle. Grandmother Moon is inviting, mysterious and powerful. She controls the tides of the seas, illuminates our way at night and possesses the power to darken the light of the sun.

There are thirteen moons in the Medicine Wheel. Each of them falls into a particular Cardinal direction: East, South, West, North.

The East represents a time of new beginnings, change, growth and hope. And this direction brings forth the New Buds Moon, the Planting Moon, and the New Flowers Moon.

The South is a time of manifestation and understanding, and where we learn to embrace life and enjoy the fullness of the day. This direction brings the Hot Sun Moon, the Hot Winds Moon, and the Harvest Moon.

The West represents a time of healing and completion, a time of maturity and the insight that all this brings. This direction holds the Hunters Moon, the First Freeze Moon, and the Silent Snow Moon.

In the North, we're connected with a time of contemplation and grounding – learning to go deep within ourselves to find our connection with the Universe. Here we find the Contemplation Moon, the Deep Snow Moon, and the Strong Winds Moon.

The Meaning of the Moon in other Cultures

Pick your era in history or your spot on the globe and you will find a culture that uses the moon as a symbol, particularly the crescent moon. The most obvious example is the yellow crescent moon associated with Islamic tradition, but there are numerous precedents to this practice, both in religion and in secular society. There is also brewing debate among some faiths over whether the moon should be considered a positive symbol.

Historians have found usage of the crescent moon image in ancient central Asian cultures that worshipped celestial gods. Long before Islamic moon symbolism, the Byzantines commonly used the image of a crescent moon. This practice was popular at the time the Turks conquered Constantinople. The Turks then adopted the crescent moon as a symbol, which some interpret as not strictly religious but as an allusion to the concepts of knowledge, light and progress. During the Ottoman Empire, people began to associate the crescent moon with the Muslim faith.

Many depictions of the Virgin Mary in classical art have her standing on a crescent moon. This inclusion of the waning or the waxing moon often symbolizes fertility. Like moon iconography in many cultures, it alludes to natural phenomena such as the ebb and flow of the tides or the cycle of the changing of seasons. Pagans also have adopted the crescent moon as an icon of their beliefs, harking back to its use by ancient pagans and polytheists.

People who have studied the era of the Ottoman Empire relate a legend that Osman, the empire's founder, dreamed of a crescent moon that encompassed the opposite ends of the earth. He saw this dream as a message of his power and potential, and decided to use the crescent moon as an icon representing his dynasty. The five-pointed star that is occasionally pictured with the crescent moon may allude to the five pillars of Islam.

Muslims diverge on the issue of whether the crescent moon truly represents their faith. In the earliest incarnations of the Muslim faith, there was no symbol used; only flags to identified believers. After the Turks took Constantinople in the 1400s, they adopted this imagery and used it on their flag. During the ensuing centuries, the Ottoman Empire retained this imagery and many outsiders came to associate the crescent moon with the Muslim faith. Some Muslims refuse to associate the moon with their beliefs because they consider the crescent moon more of a pagan icon.

The Moon in Myth and Folk Culture

The Moon has figured prominently in various mythologies and folk beliefs. The numerous lunar deities are often female such as the Greek goddesses Selene and Artemis, their Roman equivalents Luna and Diana, or the Thracian Bendis. However males are also found, such as Nanna or Sin of the Mesopotamians, Thoth of the Egyptians, and the Japanese god Susanowo.

The words lunacy, lunatic and loony are derived from Luna because of the folk belief in the Moon as a cause of periodic insanity. Folklore also stated that lycanthropes such as werewolves and weretigers, mythical creatures capable of changing form between human and beast, drew their power from the Moon and would change into their bestial form during the full Moon.

Reaching the Moon

For centuries, countries around the world have dreamed of reaching the moon. One country has realized this dream – and that moment was shared by many around the world. And now, we're dreaming even bigger – of a day that human life will be able to survive on the moon for an extended period of time.

In cartoons and comic books, we've seen artists illustrate their visions of what it would be like if humans lived on the moon. Like the stars in the sky, we feel it's just within our reach.

Because it's the Earth's only natural satellite, the moon has become a part of all of us – no matter where we live in the world. It shines in the night sky, giving us hope for the future and we are graced by its special light.

Children are in awe of the moon. It is alluring, mysterious and special. And this feeling is captured in storybooks around the world. It brings us a sense of peace when we go to sleep at night.

Moonlight Musings

Think back to your childhood and your earliest thoughts about the moon.

What did it symbolize to you? Did it factor into your childhood dreams in any way?

Take some time to write about it here.

Chapter Five

The Power of the Moon: Astrological Influences in Spiritual Transformation

The celestial bodies are the cause of all that takes place in the sublunar world.
~ Thomas Aquinas

☾

Astrology is the art of interpreting the movements of celestial bodies in relation to their links with life on earth. Most people are aware of at least one aspect of astrology – that which involves a person's sun sign. The sun takes a whole year to move around the zodiac – which is a collection of 12 constellations in the sky, taking a month to move through each of the zodiac signs.

You probably know about the characteristics of your sun sign and can apply them to your individual personality. But true astrology takes into account the positions of all the planets – and especially the moon. It is said in astrology that an individual will respond intuitively and instinctively to situations in a manner typical of their Moon sign. The Moon's position in the sky during birth sheds light on the interior life of a person and can explain why two people with the same Sun sign can be so different.

Using the Moon as a Source for Transformation

Like the moon, we all go through cycles in our lives. We have ups and downs, we go forward and back – and sometimes we seem to circle back around. We may hide behind the clouds or peek from beneath the clouds. But eventually, with support and self-confidence, we get to a point where we're able to beam with full light.

In astrology, the moon represents your true feeling nature – that which is concealed beneath the surface. Its influence in a personal birth chart illuminates your natural gifts, needs, emotions, and your style of relating to people and life scenarios. With guidance from the moon, an understanding of your emotional nature will unlock the door to your deepest feelings and hidden desires.

By exploring the meaning of the moon in an astrology chart, you can begin to answer life's vital questions: How do you naturally give and receive love? What are your natural defense mechanisms? What are you looking for in relationships?

The moon's sign in your astrology chart gives insight into your natural gifts and the ways you instinctively seek security. It is also an indicator of your strengths as a mother, and where you may be more challenged as you parent your children.

Looking at the Moon in an Astrology Chart

In order to understand moon astrology, it is important to know what the "moon sign" was at the time of your birth. When you were born, the moon (as well as the sun and the other planets) was in one of the signs of the zodiac. In contrast to the sun, the moon takes only two and a half days to move through an entire astrological sign. This means that your moon sign is more specific, making you the interesting, complex person that you are.

The location of the moon in an individual chart can reveal many things. First, we take into account the astrological sign of the moon. This is an indicator of an individual's emotional nature, as well as the relationship one may have with her mother and the type of mother she will be to her own children.

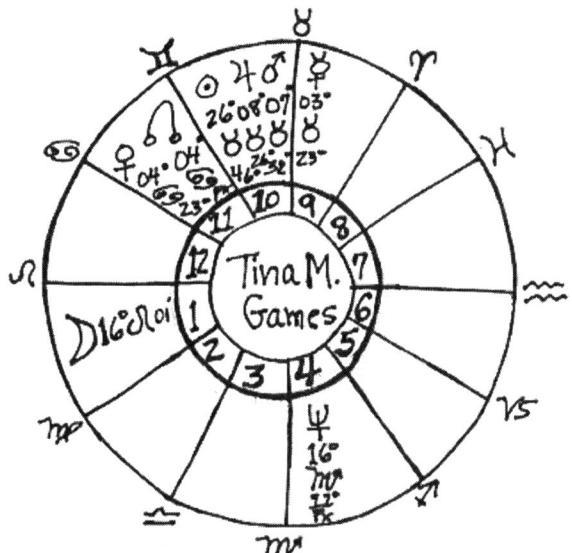

Astrology chart provided by Beverly Down, Creative Life Coach, www.StarCreativityCoaching.com

Secondly, we look to see what astrological house the moon falls in. This can give us clues as to what it is that will provide us a sense of emotional well-being. This combined with the emotional nature of the moon's astrological sign can highlight areas that need to be in alignment in order for us to feel emotionally stable.

Looking at an astrological chart, there are 12 houses. Each house represents an area of our life:
- House of Self (1st)
- House of Resources (2nd)
- House of Communication and Perception (3rd house)
- House of Home and Family (4th)
- House of Creativity, Play, and Self-Expression (5th)
- House of Health (6th)
- House of Relationships (7th)
- House of the Inner Psyche and Transformation (8th)
- House of Travel, Education, and Religion (9th)
- House of Career (10th)
- House of Friends, Hopes, and Wishes (11th)
- House of Spiritual and Transcendent Life (12th)

And thirdly, we look to see what other astrological signs are influencing the moon. What sign is ruling the house that the moon signs falls in? And what other planets are located inside a particular astrological house. A person's emotional make-up will be enhanced by these planetary energies.

The Meaning of the Moon Sign

There are many influences on a person's emotional nature, but the astrological moon sign will always represent the core emotional energy – and everything else will bounce off of that. The moon sign, at its core, will govern the way a person reacts to needs and feelings. It also applies to moods, intuitions, irrational impulses and perceptions – and it is linked to the way one loves, nurtures and plays. The moon sign is the default personality – which is your nature in moments of relaxation and also in times of stress. It's your instinctive personality – the way you are when you're not thinking about who you are.

As an example, I have a Leo moon. In a nutshell, people with Leo moons are intelligent and strongly emotional and will march to the beat of their own drum. They relish being the center of attention and have quite a lot of difficulty when they're not. A person with a moon in Leo is exceedingly charming with an exceptional sense of humor. They are leaders, not followers. However, this Moon possesses a dramatic flair and tends to take life too seriously.

Now knowing this about myself (and I will attest to the truth of it) and applying it to my role as a mother, I have had to catch myself in certain situations when my kids needed to experience things in their own way. I have a tendency to race in and make things right, rather than let a school project turn out as it may. I have to remember, it's not me in the spotlight, it's my kids – and they need to shine in their own way. And as a mother, I've had to separate their stuff from mine, so that we all are operating as individuals.

On an emotional level, with moon in Leo, I have strong reactions to things and have strong opinions. And I've had to work hard on keeping them in check so that I can hear the voices of others before passing any kind of judgment. Life is easier when I remember to take a deep breath – and not over-react. It's not an easy thing to do, but it's something that I'm aware of and something that I constantly have to make note of.

A Quick Look at the Moon Signs

Do you know what your moon sign is? If not, take a look at an ephemeris (a source that records the positioning of celestial bodies on any given day and time) and locate the day and year you were born. In some cases, you may need your birth time – if the moon was transitioning from one astrological constellation to the other at the time you were born.

Here's a quick overview of the astrological meanings of having a moon in a particular astrological sign:

Air – Gemini, Libra and Aquarius

The astrological moon signs of Gemini, Libra and Aquarius are a little different from the Sun signs because they deal with the emotions and feelings of a person. For instance, Gemini likes to acquire as much information as they can about a given situation and let others know what they have learned. Their moon sign makes them avid talkers who are prone to talking through their emotions.

Libras can please and appease. People born under this astrological moon sign have a deep need to be accepted. They tend to be crowd pleasers, but they're fairly balanced and make excellent diplomats. When it comes to their emotional nature, Librans like to talk difficulties out and abhor any perceived injustices.

Aquarians think first, then verbalize to come to a good understanding. They are well known for their emotional detachment and are not at all the jealous type. They believe strongly in honesty and trustworthiness.

Fire – Aries, Leo and Sagittarius

Aries, Leo and Sagittarius have their own way of reacting to their feelings when the moon is in the fire sign. Aries are self-assured and trust in other people's competence. They can easily become bored, so they like to keep things exciting. But they are honest about how they feel – what you see is what you get.

Anyone with a moon sign in Leo craves attention and has a flair for dramatizing. But they are very deeply passionate when expressing emotion. Leo moons are very driven, energetic, determined, exciting and romantic. Naturally charismatic, these people are natural leaders and may find themselves taking control of emotional situations.

Those with a moon in Sagittarius have a strong need for independence. They like to be able to move around and explore, and don't like being emotionally bound. They attract friends effortlessly and they're always willing to lend a helping hand.

Earth – Taurus, Virgo and Capricorn

The earth signs of Taurus, Virgo and Capricorn go through different emotions. Those with a moon in Taurus will try to defuse unwelcome situations because they like calm. They are strong, determined and very sensual people who make great friends, despite their stubbornness and their habit of challenging their romantic relationships.

Virgo moons are organizers. They like to find out what is going on by engaging in activities while determining what's happening. Sociable and clear-headed, Virgo moon signs can be critical of others and very opinionated, but this is really just their way of showing love. Look past their critical nature, and you'll find a moon sign that truly would do anything for you.

Those under the moon sign of Capricorn tend to control emotions. They tend to keep their feelings to themselves, making this the most complicated moon sign of all. Strong, stable and secure, Capricorn moon signs project an air of confidence and can-do spirit. When it comes to their feelings, these moon signs are not fickle. If they say they love you, they mean it.

Water – Cancer, Scorpio and Pisces

For the astrological moon signs of Cancer, Scorpio and Pisces, emotional expression becomes a must. Their sign makes them want to take care of – and be taken care of. Their free expression of emotions becomes extremely important.

Those in the moon sign of Scorpio can hold resentment for a lifetime if their emotions are not released. Scorpio moon signs can be perceived as cold and calculating. But if the truth be told, they are only trying to protect their feelings. They're particularly choosy when it comes to inviting others into their lives. They tend to be secretive with how they're feeling. But once they open up, they reveal very strong emotions and can be quite sensual.

Pisces moon signs want to make the world a better place, and they'll make the necessary sacrifices to do so. They are caring individuals who can show a tenderness when helping other people in need. They're loyal and have big imaginations. But they're also the most secretive of all the moon signs, preferring to hold their hearts close to the vest.

Cancer moons tend to live inside their own heads to a degree. They're sensitive and have great memories, but they are sometimes hesitant to venture outside of their imaginations. Just as people with their sun sign in Cancer, people with their moon sign in Cancer tend to enjoy being at home.

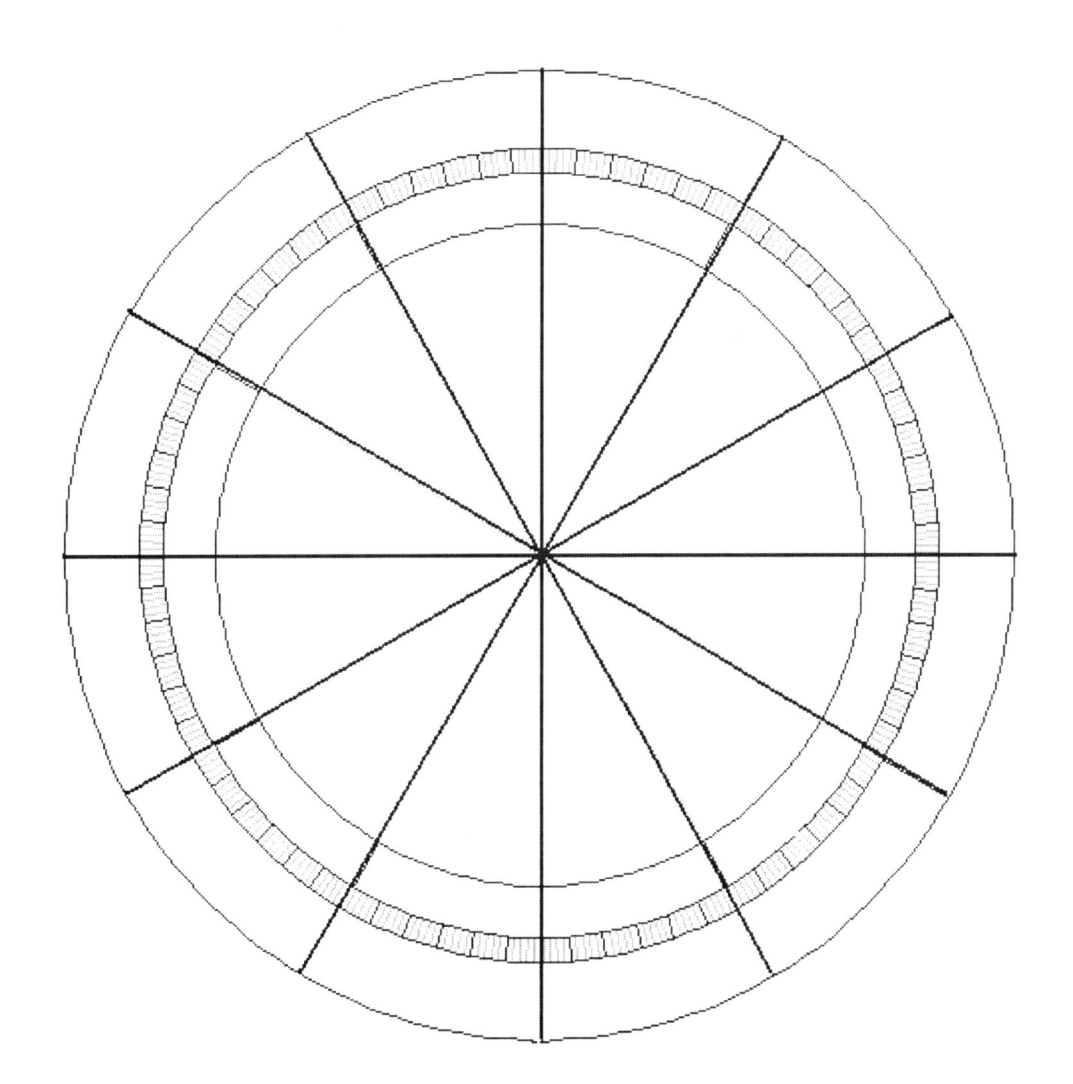

You can map out your astrological chart here.

Moonlight Musings

Take some time to find out which astrological sign rules your moon. You can find this information in an ephemeris or on an online astrology website by providing your birth information (date, time, and place).

You can also e-mail your birth information to me and I'll provide you with a synopsis of your moon sign energy. My contact information can be found in the back of this book in the "About the Author" section.

Once you locate your moon sign, make a note of that particular energy. Does it resonate with you in any way? If so, take a few minutes to write about it here.

Chapter Six

The New Moon:
The Beginning of a Quest for Self-Discovery

People are like stained-glass windows. They sparkle and shine when the sun is out, but when the darkness sets in, their true beauty is revealed only if there is a light from within.
~ *Elizabeth Kubler Ross*

☾

On the Motherhood Journey

Motherhood is an ongoing transition. Just when you think you've got it nailed, something else pops up and throws you off track. And many times during the journey, your personal identity is up for grabs – unless you reclaim it.

"I never realized just how much of my identity was wrapped up in my children until they all grew up and went about their adult lives," shared Elizabeth, a mother of three boys. "My life had been consumed with care-taking, school activities and baseball games. And when the moment came when my sons no longer needed my hand-holding, I broke down in tears. I didn't know what I would do with myself. How would I spend my days without them to take care of? I didn't know who I was anymore. It seemed like I had no purpose, no reason to get up in the morning. I was totally disconnected from myself."

It's not uncommon for moms to find themselves in total darkness when they're not able to fulfill their own passions and tend to their own self-care. It can be a never-ending cycle until the moment a light appears. When a mother realizes that her own sense of self-worth is important, everything changes – for the good.

Martha, a mother of four, fell into what she described as "a black hole." Her life had become all about taking care of her kids. "I loved my kids dearly. But I had no time to spend with myself. Anything that I was ever passionate about just got thrown to the wayside. I started falling deeper and deeper into depression. It was a really miserable place to be."

All of us have a purpose for being here on this earth. And it's perfectly normal not to be totally fulfilled by one's children. Motherhood may only be part of our purpose – and that is okay.

The New Moon

As we look at the phase of the new moon, which is the dark moon – a period of time when it is not illuminated by the light of the sun – we begin to explore our current life status, which is an awareness that a change is on the horizon. The new moon can reveal potential emotional pitfalls, as well as possibilities of how we can regain our balance.

This phase represents a time for retreating and withdrawal from the outside world. During the darkness, it's an opportunity to reflect on who we are – underneath the layers of life. It's a time to turn within and write about our inner thoughts and feelings. This is a potent time for both reflection on and acting upon soul desire. The new moon offers us the occasion and a divinely supportive opportunity to share our dreams with the power of our voices – our vehicles for expressions and co-creation.

But it's not without its discomfort. Any uneasiness over the thought of moving forward will be revealed in the new moon phase. We may feel a push/pull effect as we confront the change that is taking place within us and around us.

Moonlight Musings

Sit or stand comfortably in front of a mirror for 15 minutes. Take a good, long look at yourself. What do you see? Make a mental note of anything that you are particularly drawn to and why. Then ask yourself, "How did I get to this place in my life? How do I feel about being in this place?" And see what comes to you in thought.

Now transfer your mental notes to this page and begin to write. What did you see? What did you hear? Did any emotions arise as you looked at yourself? What were these emotions? Did they affect the way you were looking at yourself? If so, please elaborate.

Staring into Darkness

During a new moon phase, the sky is completely black, with the exception of little sparkles of light in the form of stars. It's the point in every month when the moon takes a retreat and begins to grow again, redoubling her light and reflecting new creative energy on all worldly things. This is a time to ponder where you came from, how you got to where you are now and where to go from here. It's a time to explore new ways of thinking and to prepare for a new path of travel.

This phase marks the ideal time for connecting with our inner selves and our heart's desire. By looking for the "light" and knowing that it's there, somewhere, waiting to be discovered – we can face our "dark moon" and reach a place where our personal reflection begins to shed its own light.

This is a time where dots start to connect and patterns start to reveal themselves – just as the stars do in the night sky. Everything has a place and everything has a purpose. Now it becomes our job to find our place in the next phase of life's journey.

The energies of the dark moon can feel especially potent. That's because they are. They represent the unknown and can send a magnetic pull to lure our willingness and our desire to find out – "What is it on the other side that is waiting for me?"

Moonlight Musings

Turn off the lights in whatever room you choose and sit quietly for 15 minutes with this question, "As I sit in complete darkness with the knowing that a change is on the horizon, what is it that bubbles to the surface?"

Now light a candle or turn on a very soft light. Position yourself comfortably in front of the candle or light and gaze into it for 15 minutes – and ask yourself, "What do I see in my future?"

Pay attention to any emotions that come up as you ponder your future – both immediate and down the road.

After 15 minutes, turn on a brighter light and begin to write in your journal.

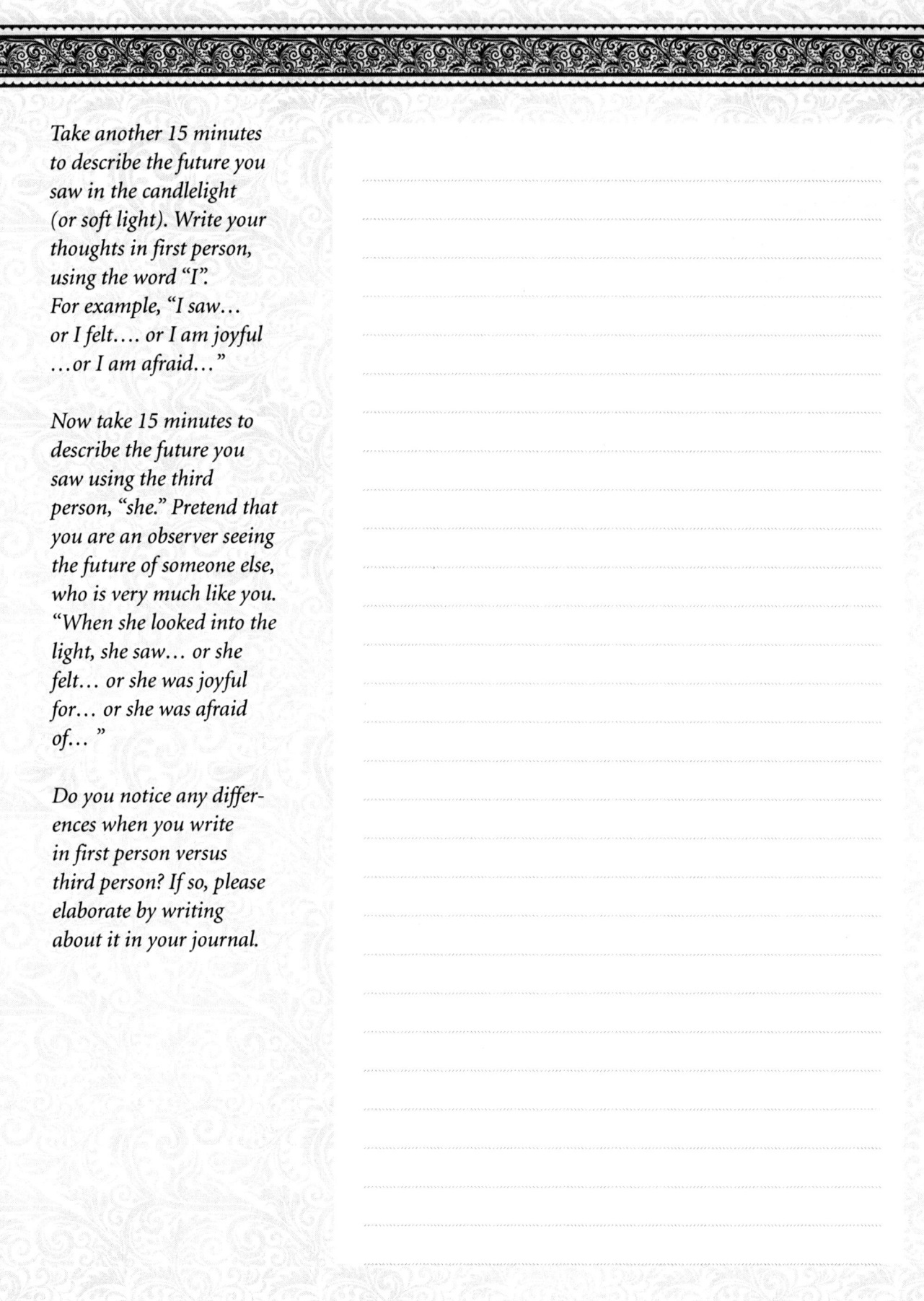

Take another 15 minutes to describe the future you saw in the candlelight (or soft light). Write your thoughts in first person, using the word "I". For example, "I saw… or I felt…. or I am joyful …or I am afraid…"

Now take 15 minutes to describe the future you saw using the third person, "she." Pretend that you are an observer seeing the future of someone else, who is very much like you. "When she looked into the light, she saw… or she felt… or she was joyful for… or she was afraid of… "

Do you notice any differences when you write in first person versus third person? If so, please elaborate by writing about it in your journal.

Chapter Seven
The Waxing Crescent
Who Are You, Really?

*Always be a first-rate version of yourself, instead of
a second-rate version of somebody else.*
~ *Judy Garland*

When Betty, a good friend of my father's, asked me at a family wedding, "So what are you doing now?" – I completely froze. I had no clue what to say. I was six months pregnant with my second child at the time and had been out of the workforce for two years. I had chosen, for better or worse, to be a stay-at-home Mom, although I never really stayed at home since I was involved with several community organizations as a volunteer.

Luckily for me, Betty sensed my discomfort and chose to rephrase her question, "What would you like to be doing?" Much to my surprise, bells went off in my head and I started rattling off a "to do" list.

It became clear to me, after that encounter, that my identity had always been tied into my career. Without it, I didn't know who I was. I was a mother, but who was I really?

Women face these types of scenarios all the time. We wear many different labels in our lives. We may be a wife, a mother, a grandmother, a teacher, a loyal employee, a neighbor – but who are we when we strip ourselves of these exterior labels? How would we describe ourselves from the inside? What passions lie within us that determine what actions we take on the outside?

Moonlight Musings

Imagine yourself in a dark room in the middle of the night. You are resting comfortably on a chair or on a bed and you have several blankets laying on top of you.

Think of the blankets as the many layers of your life. Each blanket represents a piece of your life – your health, your spirituality, your family, your career, your friends, your volunteer commitments, your hobbies, your romantic life – any areas of your life that are significant to you. Make a list of these blankets. How many do you have?

After making your list, imagine yourself being covered with these blankets. How do you feel with these blankets on top of you? Do you feel warmth? Do you feel comfort? Do you feel secure? Do you feel constrained? Do you feel smothered?

Take 20 minutes to write about the feeling of these blankets. Are any of them particularly heavy – perhaps a thermal blanket? Are any of them comfortable – perhaps a down comforter or a light quilt with just enough coverage? Are any of them particularly light – not enough material to cover your needs?

Moonlight Musings

Now slowly remove each blanket, one by one, until nothing is there but you. Without all of the layers of your life, who are you?

And how do you feel once these blankets are removed?

Describe yourself at your very core and record it in your journal.

The Waxing Crescent

In astrology, the moon is significant. It has a major influence on our emotions and can lead to a better understanding of our inner being. Who are we underneath all the layers – and how emotionally are we connected to that part of us?

As we watch the magnificent waxing and waning of the silvery white circle in the night sky, we can sense our own transformations taking place. It's during this phase that we can see the moon starting to peek out from beneath the layers of darkness.

Approximately every three to four days after the true dark of the moon, you will see a tiny sliver of a moon, like a fingernail, appearing in the sky at sunset. Imagine this fingernail as your inner being, scratching to get out.

During the phase of the waxing crescent, there's a strong need to expand the understanding we have of ourselves – and it helps to look at things from a fresh perspective. It's a time to make decisions about who we are and begin to put realizations into motion.

Astrologers have long associated the moon with maternal energy. It brings out the feminine side of our nature – the need to nurture and be nurtured. And the different phases provide different levels of connecting with our inner self.

The moon is the "night you" – when you have less distractions and more time for reflection. So it makes perfect sense that we would be more connected with our own process of transformation at a time when much of the world is asleep.

A new moon represents darkness. It's what's hidden from the world. Once we connect with that dark side and begin to accept it, we can start the process of self-discovery – making a connection with who we really are. And just as important, we must be aware of who we are not – by paying attention to what it is that's smothering us or holding us back.

The Woman in the Moon

We've all heard the saying "the man in the moon." But what exactly does that mean?

By using analogies related to the moon, a "new you" begins to emerge as life's many layers are peeled off slowly. And what emerges is the first crescent after the new moon – a peek at what's to come. By taking this analogy, we can begin to see the brightness shining from underneath all the rubble. This is our inner light. And all of a sudden, we become that woman in the moon – a woman with a very unique face, a face that we can call our own.

When you look at a waxing crescent moon, you can see the tip of a face that's beginning to emerge. The dark side of the moon is to your left, and the bright crescent is to your right. Sometimes the moon is tipped a little, so it may not be exactly right or left, but you'll be able to see the resemblance of a face that's about to make its entrance into the world. It marks the beginning of a "rebirth."

Letting go of old ways of thinking – and opening up to new ways of thinking – begins with the waxing crescent moon. You begin to notice life from a new perspective. What you conceived during the phase of the new moon, is now in the process of waxing or gestating.

Moonlight Musings

As you step out from beneath the layers of life, make your way to a mirror and look at yourself. Sit or stand comfortably in front of this mirror for 15 minutes.

Gaze deeply into your eyes (and only your eyes) and make a connection with the person who is there, staring back at you.

What do you see?

What do you hear?

What are you feeling?

What is the message that your soul is trying to send to you – without any filters – and perhaps with a new twist?

Who Are You, Really?

While many women thrive on their motherhood status and are content with it, others feel a strong need to have a personal identity beyond their role as a mother.

Laura recalled the first time someone asked her for her business card after she had made the decision to be a stay-at-home Mom. "I had this wonderful conversation with a woman on the playground about international trade. The conversation went so well that the woman wanted to have coffee and discuss it further. When she asked if she could have my card, I found myself stuttering the words, 'Well, um, I, um, let's see, um' – before I could finally get the truth out that I was no longer in the workforce. I had a really hard time admitting that. After all, not only had I been a successful career woman for 15 years, I had a Harvard MBA."

Becoming a mother is a huge life transition. Experts say that a typical adult transition takes between one and three years before one fully assimilates a new identity. So it's perfectly normal to grieve the life we had before having our children – and to miss parts of it. And it's perfectly normal to crave those things that made us happy.

Aside from our roles as mothers, we are individuals with interests, passions and desires. To be the best mothers we can be, we must grant ourselves permission to listen to the messages coming from our inner being. These are messages that tell us who we really are – at our core.

Understanding and Accepting Who We Are

When Hillary Clinton was frowned upon for her comment about not being the kind of woman who would stay at home and bake cookies, it became clear to me that all women have their own versions of happiness. Those who know what their definition of happiness is, have the better chance of enjoying motherhood to the fullest extent. While some desire the career route, others prefer to be full-time mothers. There are also many mothers who want both – a career and an opportunity to be a stay-at-home Mom. But can a woman truly have it all?

In order to find the answers, mothers need to look inward. What is it that will make you most happy?

Moonlight Musings

Let's do an exercise using a journaling technique called "springboards." This is a technique using thought-provoking questions designed to "springboard" you into the pages of your journal. Here are the questions:

If there were no obstacles regarding financial income for your family and you could have the ideal childcare arrangement, describe the choices you would make. And for mothers with adult children, flashback to a time when you feel you could have benefitted from having more personal freedom.

Let's imagine that you're setting up the ideal schedule for one full year. Would you work outside the home, full-time or part-time, doing something that you love? What would you be doing? Or would you prefer to devote your time being a full-time mother?

If so, would you consider having a childcare provider for any length of time? If the answer is yes, how long would you want the children to be in the care of the provider? And what would you do with your time – housework, errands, casual time with friends, personal projects (such as hobbies or taking classes/workshops), volunteer work? Please don't limit yourself to the choices I've given. List anything that comes to mind.

JOURNALING BY THE MOONLIGHT
A Mother's Path to Self-Discovery

Moonlight Musings

Now – with the previous answers in mind – describe what an ideal day would be like given the choices you've just listed. Factor in your children, significant others, pets, anyone or anything that would affect this scenario from the time you wake up in the morning until the time you go to sleep at night.

Moonlight Musings

Have these writing exercises shown you anything?

When we removed the obstacles of family finances and childcare arrangements, what were you left with?

Did you find yourself in that dream job? If so, what was that dream job?

If you pictured yourself staying at home with the kids full-time, did you find that you needed a break of some sort? If so, how long of a break did you need and how did you spend it?

Did a hobby or an interest in something factor into the picture? Or did you see yourself doing a little bit of both — having a career and spending time at home with the kids?

Take a few minutes to write about what came up for you during this visioning process — and identify the scenario that you most connected with.

Making a Connection between Reality and Desire

Whatever the scenario presented for you, it probably spoke to your true self – that which makes you most happy. If what you pictured in this exercise is not how you're currently living, then chances are you're feeling unfulfilled. If so, that's okay! There are ways to work through these things, little by little.

The first step is to be honest with yourself. What is it that you really want out of life? What goals or intentions would you like to set for yourself? What changes would you need to make in your life in order to obtain these things? What small step can you take today to move closer to your intentions? These are questions that we'll be exploring in the chapters ahead.

But for now, know that studies have shown that a happy mother makes the best mother. It's important to keep in mind that what makes one mother happy, might make another miserable. It's not for anyone to judge anyone's decisions or situations. As mothers, we all make sacrifices for our families. The key is to not make too many or else, they could backfire.

Patricia, a mother of three, described the first two years of motherhood as pure bliss. But by year four, she felt isolated and resentful. "My husband and I had planned for a large family. It's what both of us were accustomed to. I made the decision to leave my full-time job to stay at home with our kids. At first, I was happy with that decision. We spent time at the playground and had picnics together. I joined other Moms for playdates and coffee. I was happy with my routine until my third child arrived. Then it became too much. We were miles away from our extended families and could only afford an occasional babysitter, so I was unable to take the breaks that I desperately needed. My husband had a job that involved travel. Whenever he was away, I felt totally exhausted and angry. I felt like I had nothing in my life other than my kids. I needed something else – something to call my own."

Based on my own experience, I've learned that we can still be good mothers and love our careers or want to further our education or perhaps, pursue a hobby. We need encouragement from others who understand our situations without making us feel guilty about the choices we make.

If we are connected with our inner being, then the other phases of transformation will flow in sync – just as they do with the moon. The moonlight becomes brighter and brighter as our steps toward fulfillment become bigger and more encompassing.

Connecting with your Authentic Self

In order to fully hear the message that our soul is sending, we must loosen the reins of our outside filters. Like a new baby who enters the world without any awareness of constraints – letting go of anything we consider excess baggage can open us up to receiving the gifts that our inner being has to offer.

In order to fully embrace ourselves at our very core, we may need to step outside the box and listen to the words being shared with us by a new voice – our inner voice, which has been with us all along.

Chapter Eight
The First Quarter
Dealing With Mother's Guilt and Resentment

No one can make you feel inferior without your consent.
~ Eleanor Roosevelt

Who Decides What's Best for Us?

I will always remember that first and best piece of advice on motherhood – when my obstetrician told me, "Remember, if Mama ain't happy, nobody's happy."

Her voice rang in my ears during those first two years of motherhood. I had so many happy days with my son, being a stay-at-home mom. But I also had many more days where I felt lonely, disconnected and miserable. She convinced me that the best thing for any child is a happy mother. I attempted to live by these words, but circumstances beyond my control led to several years of mothering against the current. And to make matters worse, I felt an overwhelming sense of guilt about the negativity that I was feeling inside. I felt ashamed and fearful that someone would find out how I was really feeling – and I worried that they would judge me as an unworthy mother.

Keeping these feelings locked inside for several months, I eventually gravitated toward a black hole of darkness where I felt very alone and disconnected from anything that didn't involve my son. There were many times where I felt it was truly just he and me against the world.

As I look back on that time in my life, I knew that being a stay-at-home mom was the right thing to do for my son. But it wasn't necessarily the right thing to do for me. And sadly, it became the beginning of a two-year struggle with depression, which was filled with resentment toward my husband. While I had to adjust my life to accommodate our son's needs, he kept climbing up the corporate ladder. And that was really hard for me to swallow.

Moonlight Musings

Using a journaling technique called "captured moment" – can you recall a time in your life when you made a decision, not based on your own needs and desires, but based on the wishes or needs of someone else?

Imagine a camera snapping that moment in time – a photograph that you will forever keep embedded in your mind. It captures the emotion, the sights, the sounds, the smells – everything that took place in that moment when your life took a different turn – in a direction that you felt totally unprepared for – and quite possibly, didn't want.

Take 20 minutes to describe that moment in time and how it affected your life.

Feeling the Guilt

When Lisa, a mother of two, had to leave for a week-long business trip, she felt an overwhelming sense of guilt. She had made several after school playdates for her oldest daughter and had taken advantage of the maximum hours at her youngest daughter's daycare. It was a difficult week for her husband to leave work early, so she had no choice but to rely on other people to fill in the voids of childcare for her daughters.

"I barely enjoyed my trip because I was so worried about the feelings of my girls. We had gone over what the schedule would be while I was away and I could see the anxiety in their eyes. This was a new experience for them. It was especially unfortunate that my trip coincided with a big presentation that my husband had at work. I wanted so badly to cancel my trip, but it was something that I had to do for my job."

Working mothers face these types of challenges all the time. Mixed with the responsibilities they have to their children are the commitments they have to their careers.

But they are not alone. Stay-at-home mothers deal with guilt as well.

Amy, a mother of three, recalls, "I typically spend seven days a week, twenty-four hours a day with my children. I was desperate for a block of time to call my own. I finally gave in to a schedule that included two afternoons a week of babysitting, only to feel guilty about the money spent for the sitter. I had a hard time justifying it since I wasn't working. I also felt guilty about the time I was spending away from my children."

All mothers have experienced some form of guilt – whether it's a feeling that they haven't done enough for their child or a feeling of guilt over choosing to do something for themselves without their child.

The First Quarter

Looking into the night sky and seeing a moon half lit reminds us of what's to come. In personal transformation, we can choose to look at this moon phase as half full – or half empty.

It's hard to look at the brightness of this magnificent lunar object and not feel a sense of wonderment. There are so many possibilities in territories not yet explored. Of course, it's only natural to wonder what craters or bumpy roads may lay ahead as the moon slowly reveals itself – and as we slowly reveal our many layers.

The first quarter moon can bring up tension as it signals the balance between light and dark. The moon in this phase is half light, half dark. Obstacles to the new incoming awareness will show themselves now and feelings of guilt or resentment may emerge.

If we can apply the "moon half full" concept, we are giving ourselves permission to move ahead in this exploration of new frontiers – with a trust that we will indeed overcome any obstacles that may enter our path.

As the "new you" begins to reveal itself in the moonlight, it is common for mothers to associate any personal needs with guilt. Society puts a lot of pressure on mothers to put family first. This pressure often comes from well-intentioned individuals who don't fully understand that in order for a mother to be at her best, she needs to fulfill her own needs and desires.

As a result, a mother's needs are often pushed to the back of the line – for a time when everyone else is asleep. This is why many mothers do their best thinking at night, a time when the moon offers much comfort in a quiet, undisturbed world that's otherwise in the dark.

Accepting the Guilt for What It Is

Guilt is a normal emotion for any mother. But how does this make us feel? Should we feel guilty about putting our own needs front and center? Is it okay if we secretly resent those around us who aren't struggling with guilt the way we are?

The key is to be able to acknowledge our feelings for what they are and to learn from the lessons they bring us. When we can let go of guilt and resentment, the quality of our emotional life begins to improve and we can actually be a better, more relaxed mother.

Janet, a mother of two, remembers, "During the last trimester of my first pregnancy, my mother and my mother-in law kept reminding me about the benefits of staying home with my daughter. But it was my best friend who convinced me that I needed to do what was best for me. When I asked myself what would make me happy, the answer was keeping my career. It made me whole. I knew I could be a better mother by being a whole person rather than half a person."

So, how do mothers work through these feelings? First and foremost, we must acknowledge the guilt for what it is.

Moonlight Musings

Let's try a journaling technique using dialogue.

In your journal, you'll set up a dialogue between you and your guilt (with you playing both parts). This will look like a movie or theatre script. It may feel a little unnatural at first, like you're making things up. But that's okay! Just clear your head of any other thoughts and focus solely on whatever guilt you're feeling.

Begin by asking the question, "Why are you here?" Then close your eyes, take a deep breath and listen. Let the guilt speak. Give it plenty of time to answer. Respect the silence as the answers come to you in thought.

What does it say to you? Record the response here.

Now make a note of how this makes you feel. Respond to the answer your guilt has given you, taking time to get everything off your chest. Your guilt will then respond in turn. Let the dialogue go on as long as it needs to.

Once you feel the guilt has aired its case, ask the question, "What will it take to get you to leave me alone?" And see what comes up. Again, respect the silence and let the answers come to you in thought.

This can be a very powerful process. You may get answers and insight that seem to come from nowhere. The place they are coming from is most likely your subconscious or unconscious mind. The dialogue technique is a way to bring this information to consciousness, where it may feel unfamiliar, strange or unsettling. But trust the process!

Letting Go of Guilt

As you work through your guilt, here are some suggestions that will help in easing it:

- Focus on the positive things that you bring to your family.

- Reward yourself for a job well done.

- Recognize that you are an individual with passions and desires beyond your role as a mother.

- Take time for yourself, away from your children.

- Develop an interest or a hobby that's totally unrelated to your children.

- Create a support system that includes people who understand your parenting situation and your desire to do the best job you can with your children.

Mothering gets better and better as we become more confident with the choices we make. Let's remind ourselves that we're doing the best we can in every circumstance and allow ourselves the freedom to let go of guilty feelings. That includes letting go of any unsolicited advice.

And like the "moon half full," let's look ahead at the new frontier – the possibilities and the benefits of living a fulfilled life. The moon offers great opportunities to those who seek her wisdom and her guidance.

Moonlight Musings

Sit comfortably in a chair and close your eyes. Inhale deeply and exhale slowly.

With every breath you take, ask your inner being for her wisdom. And with every exhale, ask your inner being for her strength in letting go of any attachments to memories or emotions that only cause you pain.

Then ask yourself these questions – "What memory or feeling must I let go of in order to move my entire being toward the light of my larger purpose? And who would I be without it?"

When you're ready, open your eyes and record the answers you've been given.

Chapter Nine

The Waxing Gibbous
The Strength of a Support System

Somewhere, there are people to whom we can speak with passion without having the words catch in our throats. Somewhere a circle of hands will open to receive us, eyes will light up as we enter, voices will celebrate with us whenever we come into our own power.
~ *Starhawk*

Finding Our Tribe

No one understands a feeling or a situation any more than someone else who has been through it – or who may still be going though it. This is what "finding your tribe" means to me.

As I suffered through what could have been labeled postpartum depression – which I now think is a layer of what I call "maternal depression" – I ached for someone else who could truly empathize with the pain that I was feeling. It took a good two years for me to make a connection with other mothers who "had been there" or who "were there."

In that gap of time – before I met "my tribe" – I remember feeling like it was just my son and me against the world. It was an overwhelming feeling that totally overpowered me and sent me on a spiral into darkness. And it wasn't until I met "my tribe" that I started seeing the light again.

Kathleen Adams writes in *Scribing the Soul*, "Humans are tribal people."

Yes, we are. And in periods of pain and darkness, I think it is imperative to make that connection with "one's tribe."

My spiral of darkness brought a deep sense of pain into my life – a pain that no one else around me could understand. But my journal held that pain and allowed me to take a long hard look at it. And when I did, I started to see the little bits of light. And through the light, I started seeing this pain in other mothers. It was then that I realized – I wasn't alone.

And in those moments of light, I felt inspired because I knew there was a community of like-minded women who felt the way I did. All I needed to do was connect with them. It was this experience that has been the guiding force of the work I do now. And when I think back to that dark time in my life, it gives light to my life purpose. I would never be where I am now, had it not been for that experience. As painful as it was, it became the very foundation that I needed to "form my tribe" and to go forward with a heart filled with empathy and compassion – and a strong desire to help other mothers come out from behind the darkness of the moon.

Moonlight Musings

If you're able, take a walk outside and find a place where you can feel connected to nature. Make yourself comfortable in this space – maybe on a park bench or a picnic blanket, or on the end of a pier with your legs dangling in the water or sitting on a rock in the middle of a flower garden. Wherever you are, however you're sitting, take a long look around you and breathe in nature's wisdom.

Now close your eyes. Inhale deeply and exhale slowly – and imagine the sound of beating drums. Feel the rhythm of these drums and listen carefully for the wisdom of the Native American elders coming to you in the form of thoughts. And with these thoughts, they present you with members of your tribe.

Who do you see? Do you know these people? Are they in your life now? Or are they people you are meeting for the first time? Are any of them animals? They seem to understand you. They seem to feel your pain. They seem genuinely interested in your well-being. And what wisdom do they bring to share with you?

When you feel ready, open your eyes and describe your tribe.

A Mother's Support System

One of the most important things to a mother is having a strong support system. This can include a supportive partner, an extended family, babysitters, support groups, neighbors and friends. Mothers need people in their lives that they can trust, whether it's a confidante or someone who can help out with the children in a moment's notice.

Janice, a mother of two, realized how significant a support system can be when she was seven months pregnant with her second child. She and her husband were miles away from both of their families. "We were organizing our game plan for the arrival of our new baby. When we started discussing what would happen when my water broke, we suddenly realized that we had no one to take care of our daughter while I was in the hospital giving birth. Why we hadn't thought of that before then still baffles me to this day."

There are many reasons that every mother should have a strong support system. One of the biggest reasons is to minimize isolation. For first-time stay-at-home moms, this is crucial. There are also many mothers who don't have a local network of friends and family, due to various situations such as relocating to a new city or town.

Feeling isolated can also be a little terrifying when you're in the middle of a crisis. Not being able to have a back-up when needed can really test a mother's confidence.

Charlotte, mother of three, describes, "When we moved to the West Coast from the East Coast, I felt totally lost and alone. My husband was traveling a lot and would be gone for extended periods of time, so I had sole responsibility for the kids. I remember waking up one night and hearing my son cry. When I checked on him, he was soaking wet and felt very hot. I checked his temperature and it read 104. I gave him something to bring down the fever and quickly called the doctor. I had to wait over an hour to get a response. I must admit, I was really scared. I had no one to fall back on in the event that the doctor would have advised a visit to the emergency room. What would I have done with my other two kids? Hiked them to the emergency room, too? It was a cold, rainy night which would have made it difficult. Luckily, the doctor advised some at-home treatments until the next morning when we could make it to his office."

The Waxing Gibbous

As the moon circles the Earth, the Earth circles the Sun. It's a natural support system – and one that we take for granted every day. The moon depends on the Earth's orbit for survival. And the Earth depends on the Sun for survival. Each one plays a part in creating a "whole world."

Imagine yourself as the Earth and your child or children as the moon. And imagine that the Sun is everything that supports you – a life partner, your family, your community, your social network. Do you think you could survive without the Sun? And could the moon survive without you?

As we look at the moon in its waxing gibbous phase, we see it with three quarters of light. This light comes from the sun with the remaining one quarter being blocked by the shadow of the Earth. And what happens when the moon emerges from any blocks of light? It becomes full and rich in color – and something that is extraordinarily beautiful.

Can you imagine what it would feel like to be free of any blocks, with nothing holding you back from living a full and rich life? It's a creation of "wholeness" and the first step to a feeling of being complete.

And what would your children learn from a mother who knew how to ask for help when she needed it?

Take a look at the moon when it transitions from a waxing gibbous phase to being completely full of light. It's as if the last layer has been removed and the birth of a new moon has emerged. It's an image that is awe-inspiring.

Paying Attention to the Synchronicities

When the universe is connecting on all fronts, the law of attraction is apparent and a woman can begin to see the synchronicities in her life – and the creative manifestation can begin. We start to meet the right people. We begin to find ourselves in the right places at the right time. And doors of opportunity start to open.

"I had a hard time when I heard the words, 'Your child has some significant developmental delays.' My youngest son was three years old at the time – and the news was just too much to bear," recalls Sandy, a mother of two. "I felt all alone with no one who could understand what I going through inside. Then one day, on the way out of the doctor's office, a woman came up to me and handed me a note with her name and number. She had overheard my conversation in the hall with a nurse. She told me that she had started a support group for mothers of special needs children. My prayers had been answered!"

With a strong support system, we can minimize any stress and anxiety that may get in the way of staying true to our authentic self. When a feeling of overwhelm or depression occurs, a call to a trusted friend or family member can make all the difference.

But how can we recognize that we are connecting to the right people and the right scenarios? How do we know that we're on the right path? Can we ask the universe for signs?

This is when we need to be as specific as we can about what we desire in our lives. The more specific we can be, the more we're able to make the right connections.

Moonlight Musings

Let's begin by crafting a statement of intention. What is it that you would like to attract to you? Is it a local writing group of like-minded women? Is it someone who can connect you to the right job? Is it an article in a magazine that describes the ideal community where you could retire?

Try to be as specific as possible by keeping your statement around 25 words and making it an "I will" statement – such as, "I will make a connection with a group of like-minded women who are interested in exploring their authentic selves through journaling."

Read this statement first thing every morning and again before you go to bed.

And for the next few weeks keep a synchronicity log where you'll note anything that pops up or anyone that crosses your path who seems to connect – in one way, shape or form – with this statement of intention.

And at the end of the period, take a look at these synchronicities and see what connections they have to each other and what message they may be sending to you.

Take some time to record your thoughts here.

Minimizing Stress and Anxiety

In order for any mother to feel complete, she must develop strategies that will allow for a deep and fulfilling connection to her authentic self. Having a strong support system can minimize any stress and anxiety levels that may get in the way. When a feeling of overwhelm occurs, a call to a trusted friend or family member can make all the difference.

But what happens when a mother doesn't have that option?

Sara, a mother of two, had a perfect work opportunity that came to her just a couple of months after her kids started school. "It was a marketing position and the company was willing to let me work from home. I only had to attend two in-person meetings per month. It was a dream come true. I figured that I would schedule my in-person meetings at a time when my kids were in school. Everything went well for the first few months until one of my in-person meetings was moved to a time late in the afternoon. I tried desperately to find someone to take care of my children that day, but had no luck. I ended up having to cancel the meeting which led to the cancellation of the project. The company then decided that my work-at-home situation no longer worked for them. It wasn't something that I had anticipated. I was so disappointed that I didn't sleep for days."

Moonlight Musings

Now, let's take a look at your situation by using a journaling technique called "character sketch." With this technique, you will describe yourself, from the outside looking in, as having the ideal support system. Before you begin creating your character sketch, consider the following questions.

Are you a stay-at-home Mom? Are you a working mother? Are you a work-at-home Mom? Are you a Mom with college-aged children?

How strong is your support system? If there was an emergency, do you have someone you can call in a moment's notice to help out with your children? Who is this person? Is it easy to reach them? If, for whatever reason, they're not available, do you have a back-up?

How supportive is your spouse or partner? Are they willing to take on more of the parenting duties if you have something you need or want to do?

If you're a working mother, how flexible is your company with leave time? If you find yourself needing to take off three days in a row due to a child's illness, how will your company accommodate you? What if you need longer than three days? Do you have a plan?

If you're a stay-at-home Mom, do you suffer from isolation or a feeling of being overwhelmed? If so, have you explored what support groups are available in your area for stay-at-home mothers? Do any of these groups offer babysitting services that will allow you to have some "me" time or time to go to lunch with your husband or a new friend?

With your answers in mind, create a character sketch (in the present tense) of you having the ideal support system. If you're a working mother, describe your ideal work schedule and what you'd need from your work environment, your boss and/or your co-workers. If you're a stay at home mom, describe what you'd need in order to feel content with your everyday schedule.

For both situations, be sure to factor in the necessary breaks you need for yourself. If you're married or living with your partner, describe what you'd need from them. Also, describe your plans for emergency childcare. Remember, do this in present tense, as if it's happening now.

If you're a single parent, do you have a support system in place? If not, what do you need in order to feel at ease should an emergency arise?

Once you have your character sketch done and your ideal scenario in place, take a look at how far (or how close) you are in making that scenario real. If it's not as close as it needs to be, what will it take in order for you to create the ideal support system? Are you in a position to begin putting this ideal support system together?

Take some time to map out your thoughts here.

Creating Your Circle of Support

Putting together a circle of support provides a pillow for comfort and protection. This circle can consist of anything or anyone that can "have your back" in a moment of crisis. It can include loyal friends, devoted family members, a trusted doctor or therapist, your place of worship, your dog or cat – and your "always there when you need her" journal.

As you continue on your journey of self-discovery, think about who you can share your joys with, cry your tears with, and who (or what) will give you the space "to be you" without any form of judgment. There is no need for perfection in a circle of support. This is a place where you can be your most vulnerable and still feel loved and appreciated for who you are.

The key to eliminating mother-related anxiety and stress, is to know what resources you have available – and how to use them when the need arises. Like the light of the moon, the path becomes clearer when we recognize the strength of a support system.

Moonlight Musings

Think back to the tribe you described earlier. Now it's your turn to call them into your circle of support.

Imagine yourself in the center of this circle. The only lighting comes from the full moon in the sky above you.

Call them, one by one, into the circle and tell them what you need – and ask for their support in honoring your authentic self without any judgment.

Make a list of your support circle members and record them on this page. And make a note beside each name, listing what it is that you need from them in order to feel fully supported.

Now decorate the next page in a way that brings a calm feeling to you.

Chapter Ten
The Full Moon
Identifying Your True Self

It's a marvelous night for a moondance.
~ Van Morrison

Dancing by the Light of the Moon

For many centuries, the moon has inspired thousands of beautiful stories, songs, dances, paintings and poems. Through its many phases, it has served as a muse in a variety of ways. What is it about the moon that stirs our innermost thoughts and inspires our deepest creativity?

This poem written by Mark Heard, first appeared in his lyric collection, *Eye of the Storm* in 1982:

Moon Flower

When the moon blooms
Like a flower in the night
Petals of Heaven-born silver light
Its seeds ride the wind
To the souls of men
So silently
There is a fanfare
In the changing wind
For those who will listen
Beginning to end
And the nightingale pleads
For the well-tuned ears
Of every man

Oh the sun shines
Like a torch at sea
Author of all
For the eyes that see
Blind eyes know it only as a mystery
When the moon blooms
Like a flower in the night
Petals of Heaven-born silver light
Its seeds ride the wind
To the souls of men
So silently.

Moonlight Musings

Sit with the above poem for a few minutes, absorbing the beautifully-crafted words and picturing the images that come up for you.

And if possible, take a walk outside to view the full moon in its entirety.

If you're unable to view the full moon, try pulling up an image of it in a book or on your computer.

As you ponder the words of the poem and take in the radiant light of the full moon, what comes to mind? And how does this connect with your inner being?

Record your thoughts here and decorate the pages with colors that represent the fullness of the moon.

The Full Moon

The full moon is a time of high energy and great sensitivity. It's also a time of creativity. Dreams (both day and night) are at their height during this phase. This period acts as a bridge, taking the lessons learned from the past and projecting new ideas into the future.

What was conceived in the new moon phase can now come to fruition by being birthed into the full light of our conscious minds. This marks the ideal time to put something new into the universe.

A full moon experience can offer us greater illumination of our essential divinity. Issues that have been worked on since the new moon may now reach a climax. And if the restrictions of the past have been released during the waxing moon, then the full moon can bring fulfillment.

Here we are asked to claim the true gift of the inner refinement that the past initiatory fires of life have catalyzed, and to accept that our trials had to precede stepping forth into our greater fulfillment and destiny.

The full moon phase is the ideal time to bring the authentic self out to play. It's time to introduce her to the material world.

Connecting with Your Authentic Self

The inner voice, coming from essence, is the natural voice. And what is the sound of this natural voice? During the formative years, many children learn to fear their authentic expressiveness. They suppress themselves and learn to speak so that they can fit in and be accepted. They forfeit their true nature as they are shaped more by outer rather than inner forces.

Julie, a mother of twins, remembered her overwhelming desire to return to college when her daughters entered high school. "There was a voice inside of me, pulling me toward doing what was necessary to get into the field of publishing. I had always loved literature, even as a young girl. I was always surrounded by books and loved telling stories to my friends. I would often put together handmade books with collections of stories that I would find or that people would share with me. I knew this was my calling. But I never had the courage to pursue it until my girls were older. I was always told that I had to be a mother first. So I complied."

Parents are usually the first to welcome the voice of the child. They repeat back the baby's gibberish with approval, and the infant has its first lesson in pleasing the grandest figures of all. The infant learns – if you speak in a way that causes others to respond positively, all will be right in the world.

As children move into the classroom, teachers take the place of parents and offer a new approval system – grades. The As and the Fs further reinforce the distinction between what is right and wrong to say. In addition, they represent the power placed on evaluations made by an external, higher authority.

Thus we orphan our real voices and change in order to get along, be accepted, and remain comfortable. This fact underlies the fear of speaking our truth. It is a reluctance to be real and the insecurity about living from that authentic core that makes people afraid to stand up and speak out.

To find and reconnect with your authentic voice requires a safe haven. This is where your tribe comes in – by offering the space to freely express yourself without fear of criticism. Surround yourself with listeners who can focus positive attention and affirm who you truly are – and who can celebrate your natural aliveness. An inspired learning environment is one which gives you permission to develop at your own pace and in your own style. Make certain that the emphasis is on learning how to be yourself and how to connect to others in a genuine manner.

Remember there is a pure sense of self within everyone, and that this essential self has a voice. No matter the disconnection over time, you can reclaim that voice. It has always been there and simply needs to be welcomed back into the world. Let go of pretence and reveal yourself to others. In the presence of those who give you only appreciative feedback for your true nature, you can gently move toward and transform your fear. From this essential core, you speak with true fearless joy.

Moonlight Musings

Thinking back to your childhood – and going back as far as you can remember – what did you want to be when you grew up?

What were your natural talents and what were your interests?

What kind of books did you like to read?

What kind of games did you like to play?

Take a few minutes to write about your childhood here.

Moonlight Musings

Now invite your inner child out for a play date. Create the space that would be welcoming to her authenticity. There will be no judgments and no criticisms in this space. It's a place to "just be" and to "have fun."

On this page, draw a play area and color it with crayons or colored pencils. Give your inner child a name and invite her out to play.

And as the two of you are playing, describe your time together using single words or sentence fragments – and in no particular order and in no particular format, scatter them across this page.

Moonlight Musings

When the play date is over, thank your inner child for her visit – and write about the experience here. Record your thoughts in first person.

Creating a Purpose-Filled Life

We live in an age when many of us feel out of control, victimized by velocity and the direction of modern life. Too much seems to be happening to us that is not of our own making. We are swept along with the opinions of others and bruised by the outcome of world events. Many of us long for a life that is more handmade and more satisfying than the life we seem to be leading by default.

But what if we took a bold step by making an effort to live in the moment – in a way that feels authentic to us? One could only imagine what the world would look like if we were all given the opportunity to be our own person, form our own opinions – and live true to our heart's desire. To live in a world free of judgment and criticism would be the ultimate way to honor authenticity – in ourselves and everyone around us.

As we ponder our own purpose and the power that lives within us, the answers to our questions can be found in the heart of our authentic self. What natural talents and interests do we have? How can they be combined to bring fulfillment and meaning to our lives? And how can we apply our passions and desires to our real life work in the world?

What is it that would bring the most meaning to us, as individuals – and how can we synchronize the different areas of our lives to connect the pieces into a whole picture? What are the messages being sent by the universe that point us in the direction of our own authenticity?

Moonlight Musings

Treat yourself to a mini-getaway, even if it's just for a couple of hours. Where would you go? What would you be doing? And how would this open the door for a dialogue with your adult authentic self?

During this retreat, let's imagine that you are hanging out with your best friend – your authentic self. She doesn't want to think about obstacles. She doesn't want to think about failures. She's not concerned about money.

What is it that she would want to be doing if there were absolutely no considerations of obstacles or failures?

If she had one chance to make her impression on the universe, how would she do it – and why?

Engage in a dialogue with her. If you've given her a name previously, let her speak to you in that voice. If you have yet to name her, listen to her words of wisdom and let her tell you who she is.

Record this conversation on these pages – and make a note of any insights that came to you as she was speaking.

Chapter Eleven

The Waning Gibbous
Creating the Bigger Picture

Begin with the end in mind.
~ **Stephen R. Covey**

Pulling Together the Pieces of the Puzzle

During the full moon phase, we experienced what it would feel like if we could live an authentic, purpose-driven life. Now the full moon begins to close its curtain as it moves into the waning gibbous phase, going into a place where the groundwork is laid.

This is a time for taking action and for laying out our plans to make this way of living a reality. What would you like to see as the end result? And what are the scenarios that are needed in order to achieve it?

The idea is very simple. All great things are created twice – first in the mind and then in reality. First, we must get clear on what we want. Then we create it in reality.

Think of building a house. What's the first step? Typically, we discuss our ideas with an architect who will then create a blueprint – rather than bringing in a construction team to build it blindly.

So with this in mind, I'd like to invite you to review all the synchronicities that have occurred in the past few weeks. Go back through your Moonlight Musings and highlight them using a favorite color. What were some of the messages you received? What were some of the insights that came to you? What did you discover about yourself?

This is all part of connecting the dots and creating your personal constellation – just as the stars do in the night sky. Everything suddenly becomes part of a bigger meaning and part of a bigger message sent to you by your higher power or your inner being.

Moonlight Musings

Take a few minutes to review the journal entries you've made in this book so far – and highlight any insights, patterns and messages that make themselves visible to you. What synchronicities do you notice?

Make a new journal entry on this page and record any synchronicities you discover and ask yourself, "What connections do they have with each other?"

Moonlight Musings

With these synchronicities in mind (and with the eyes of the authentic self), jot down anything you would like to accomplish in the next 10, 20, 30+ years. Think about your life as a whole – and list everything you'd like to do, see, hear, feel, touch and taste. Feel free to include other people (and any animals) in your list.

Once you've completed your list, decorate this page with your favorite colors – and feel free to add any stickers that your inner child may be drawn to.

And for the next couple of days, take a look through a variety of magazines and printed publications – and cut out any images that you see which reflect the things on your list. With clear desires in mind, look for the exact pictures which portray your goals. For example, if you want a house by the water, then flip through the pages of a home magazine until you find something that represents that. If you want to start your own business, find images that capture that dream for you. If you want to learn how to play the guitar, then find that picture.

When you've collected enough images, put them into an envelope or tuck them inside this book. They will be needed for our next Moonlight Musing.

The Waning Gibbous

When the moon is waning, it represents a time for bearing fruit and participating with others, and letting go of any plans or old patterns that aren't in sync with the authentic self. This phase is receptive and demonstrative – and is about communication, sharing resources, and being open to transformation. It connects to the first quarter phase and also relates to the feeling-moving body. The power of what is felt to be significant is a propelling force for its distribution.

At this stage, feelings need to be shared with others. The energy of this phase pertains to motion. An offering of belief is made. There is a need to align the personal vision with the needs of the whole and to gain perspective.

During this phase, we should share our vision with the universe and ask, "How do my personal goals contribute to the welfare of the collective? Review the feelings that emerged in the first quarter phase and allow them to blossom in the waning gibbous – which can bring illumination to the influences of the entire lunar cycle.

This phase can affirm that our present world of dualities and evolutionary struggles can offer opportunities, which lead to heartfelt expansions of consciousness.

Creating the Bigger Picture

In order for our dreams to come true, we need a clear vision of what that looks like. We need the bigger vision in order to create the steps to get there.

A vision board (also called a creativity collage, a treasure map, or a visual explorer) is typically created on a foam or poster board on which you paste or collage images that you've torn out from various magazines and printed publications. The idea behind this is that when you surround yourself with images of who you want to become, what you want to have, where you want to live or where you want to vacation – your life changes to match those images and those desires. The images add feeling to your intentions and clarity to your desires.

Inspirational speaker and author Wayne Dyer says, "When you change the way you look at things, the things you look at change."

Have a little ritual before you begin creating your vision board. Light a candle, sit quietly and set the intent. With gentleness and openness, ask yourself what it is that you want. Maybe one word will be the answer. Maybe images will come into your head. Just take a moment to be with whatever pops into your mind.

This process makes it a deeper experience. It gives a chance for your ego to step aside just a little, so that you can create your vision more clearly.

The vision board, with its larger picture, will represent your personal moon in all its fullness. It will show the many pieces of the puzzle – that fit together to create one over-arching dream.

Moonlight Musings

It's time to create a vision board!

Using the law of attraction, you'll be creating a snapshot image of your hopes, dreams and desires – and sharing it with the universe (the more we share with the universe, the more it shares with us).

For this creative project, you'll need a piece of foam board or poster board, a glue stick and your magazine images.

Carefully assemble the images you've collected on your board (in a way that works for you). This will be a collage, so try not to leave any blank space on the board (every spot will be covered with an image – and images will overlap).

Once you've assembled them, glue them on the board – and put it in a place where you will see it often. The law of attraction will start to work its magic and the synchronicities will start to increase.

And take a few minutes to write about what you see – as a whole – in your vision board. Look at every inch of your board and record the first thoughts that come to your mind. The more you put these energies out into the universe, the more they manifest.

Creating a Life Purpose Statement

A life purpose is the context or vessel in which you build your life. It's this context that contains our daily lives – and shapes and directs our actions. It's a way of being or a vision that inspires what you do. And a life purpose statement puts this purpose into words.

The most powerful life purpose statements are a compilation of three elements: (1) the vision you hold for what's possible for yourself and the world; (2) your core values – what matters to you; (3) the essence of your being (who you are and what people count on from you).

As you craft your own life purpose statement, consider the following questions:

- *What do you love to do?*

- *What kind of people do you love to be with?*

- *What are some of the things you could do to give yourself the opportunity to spend more time with these people?*

- *If money, time, energy and talent were unlimited, what would you do with your life and who would you be?*

- *Who are some people that you greatly admire?*

- *What is it about these people that you admire?*

- *What values are important to you?*

Your life purpose statement will become the basis for creating a purpose-filled life. It will help guide you toward living a life filled with meaning and to make decisions from the eyes and heart of the authentic self.

Moonlight Musings

Using your vision board, create a life purpose statement (in first person) that best summarizes (or blankets) your ultimate life dream (or heart's desire). This can be one short sentence or one long sentence. It doesn't matter as long as it represents exactly what you want for the rest of your life.

As an example, my life purpose statement reads, "I intend to live a life filled with compassion, creativity, and appreciation for all that is unique and beautiful in the world – and without a need for perfection or judgment of myself or others."

Once you've developed a statement, write it on a piece of colorful paper, decorate it and paste it on the back of your vision board. This will become your mantra for daily living as you continue to absorb the images you assembled for yourself.

Write this statement again here – on this page – so you have it documented in two places.

And beware – your synchronicity antenna will be on high alert!

Chapter Twelve
The Last Quarter
Taking Baby Steps

"It is better to take many small steps in the right direction than to make a great leap forward only to stumble backward."
~ *Old Chinese Proverb*

Taking Life One Day at a Time

We've all heard the phrase, "Keep your eye on the prize."

This can be interpreted in many different ways – depending on what the "prize" means to us. But it usually requires some sort of vision that allows us to put the law of attraction to work. This vision gives us the opportunity to become more aware of the synchronicities around us – which hold messages from the universe and our inner spirit that we are, indeed, on the right path.

But when we're in the middle of a difficult transition, it's easy to get overwhelmed with the emotions of "just getting through it." That's why it's important to take a deep breath, adjust the speed in which our life is going and put the focus on living one day at a time.

Kelly describes an international family move that really triggered her anxiety. "I was completely overwhelmed with the many tasks involved in moving my family overseas. It was so intense at times, I couldn't enjoy the thought of the awesome opportunity we had been handed. The kids were so excited about the experience, but I couldn't seem to get into the groove. Then I stopped, took a deep breath and decided to take it one step at a time."

If we can do this – moment by moment, hour by hour, day by day – things begin to change. Have you ever watched a sunrise or a sunset? Have you noticed that the sun rises and sets bit by bit – and not in one fell swoop? This is nature's message to us – slow down and take it step by step, just like a baby who is learning to walk.

And with each baby step, we connect more and more with the power that's inside of us – putting us closer and closer to living an authentic life.

Moonlight Musings

As you look at the vision board that you created in the previous chapter, taking in each image and blending them into a whole – what is the first emotion that comes to mind? And how does it connect with the life purpose statement that you wrote?

With this in mind, imagine yourself in a field of wildflowers right before dawn. The moon is still in the sky and the sun is beginning to peek over the horizon. You sit quietly in the field – with the images of your vision board – and you release them into nature, one by one, like butterflies – flying high up into the sky. Each image flutters about – capturing the energy of the moon, the sun and the wildflowers.

Then they fly back down to you, bringing the magical energy and wisdom of nature. They flutter around you – wrapping you in a circle of love and authenticity. You close your eyes and receive nature's gifts – brought to you by the butterflies.

How does this feel? Does it feel safe enough to stand up and take a first step toward your bigger vision?

Write about this experience.

The Last Quarter

In the third quarter, the moon is rapidly waning towards a new phase of life. This represents a time to move beyond the past and start working toward the activation of what lies ahead.

The last quarter phase is active and responsible. It is about reorientation, transition and completion. It connects to the big picture focus of the waning crescent phase and also pertains to the instinctive body. Intuition and sensory connections are strong now and the instinctive responses to the environment direct the final actions that are necessary to the fulfillment of goals. At this stage, any action taken is either one of changing a past action, behavior or thought pattern – or the final push needed to realize a successful outcome.

The energy of this phase is stimulated by the five senses making every action essential and evident. It's an inventive time which supports the changing of a structure that has been built over time – and allows for manifestation of new visions.

In this phase, we are recognized for our accomplishments while accepting the responsibilities of our actions. We instinctively know the proper course, yet we still find ourselves asking, "Where do I go from here?"

It's now time to use what we have accomplished in the other moon phases and time to release any blocked energy that has prevented us from taking that first step.

Creating an Authentic Path

Our own transformation through the phases of the moon allows us to move beyond the words and immerse ourselves in our dreams. We are capable of active fantasy now where we can write the screenplays for our inner journeys. But it's still up to us, individually, to transform the best of our visions into something that is real.

Know that you have the wisdom and freedom to make your own choices. And know that your inner spirit is both inspiring and encouraging as you begin to seek healthy outlets for your emotions and activities.

When communicating with or seeking guidance from your authentic self, know that she:
- Affirms your spirit
- Leaves you feeling confident
- Eases your insecurities
- Elicits your compassion for those around you
- Encourages self-love and acceptance of yourself
- Is honest
- Inspires you to be more generous and courageous

As you prepare to travel on your authentic path, how does it feel to have a deeper relationship with your authentic self? How does it feel to have expanded your spiritual boundaries with her?

She makes great a travel companion, don't you think? Take her with you and give her permission to lead the way.

Moonlight Musings

Sitting with your vision board, picture each image separately – waiting for you at the end of a path, gathered together as a big basket of fruit. Each piece of fruit represents a part of you – your hopes, your dreams, your desires, your passions. And assembled together, each piece of fruit becomes part of the whole basket, wrapped together with sparkling paper and a flowing ribbon. And there it sits waiting for you – when you are ready to claim it.

Now close your eyes and imagine that the pathway, leading to the basket of fruit, is made up of cobblestones – each stone representing a small step. You feel comfortable where you are and you feel no pressure to move ahead quickly. You sit there with the first cobblestone, pondering where it might take you today. You can see the fruit basket in the distance and you know that it will be there when you get there. You feel confident and comfortable with the intention of taking one step at a time at your own pace. So you take a deep breath and take one small step forward.

As you stand on the cobblestone, breathe deeply – several times – breathing out what you left behind and breathing in the energy of what's ahead of you – in the fruit basket.

As you feel yourself beginning to connect with the energy of this first cobblestone, what images come to mind? Spend a few minutes pondering the meaning of them.

Now open your eyes.

Holding the energy of the first cobblestone – what small step can you take today that will move you toward your bigger vision? Write about this here.

Setting Intentions That Are Manageable

As we look at the cobblestones that pave the way on our authentic, moonlit path – we realize that the cumulative effect of our smaller choices is powerful and far-reaching.

We have to make our intentions manageable by detailing the specific steps that will carry us to our vision. Managing one small action at a time can reshape outcomes, reform negatives and rebuild relationships.

Moment-to-moment choices are often habitual and as telling as a fingerprint. Just as the chromosomes of a single cell are the blueprint to an entire organism, the most innocuous behaviors define the whole person. We are creatures of habit. One way to improve your life is to identify, understand and manage the patterns of thought and behavior that originally shaped it.

As we monitor these thoughts and behaviors, let's focus on the myriad of seemingly inconsequential choices we make daily. Accumulated micro-choices add up. Applying intention to those choices enables change to occur – change that allows us to live the life of our dreams.

Telling the truth about our thoughts, values, feelings, desires, beliefs and behaviors helps establish new and useful means of exploring issues and circumstances that compose our life. Such discovery is largely useless when not followed up with intentions – a commitment to specific tasks that together, build toward creating a bigger vision.

What intentions can we set toward living a purpose-filled life? What small step can we take today – and every day – that will put us closer to living the life of our dreams? How can we see the synchronicities in our life transitions and life scenarios – and how do they connect with our bigger vision?

Moonlight Musings

As you look forward on the cobblestone path, focus on the fruit basket that is waiting for you at the end. In an effort to move a little closer, what intentions would you like to set for the near future?

Think of five things that are realistic for you and write those down here.

How long do you think it will take you to realize these intentions? Would you like to commit to a date for each intention? If so, write it down.

Now look a bit further ahead. What else do you see? Are there other steps that you would like to reach – with the realization that they may take more time? If so, write them down.

Moonlight Musings

On the next page draw a sketch of a cobblestone path with a big, beautiful fruit basket waiting at the end. Inside each cobblestone, write your intentions – both in the near future and further out. Color the fruit in the basket, using your favorite colors.

Now add some grass to the path – around the cobblestones – and a moonlit sky. Will the moon be a crescent moon, a waning moon or a full moon?

When you're finished, take a look at your path and write one sentence that describes how you feel in this moment. Write this sentence at the bottom of this page.

JOURNALING BY THE MOONLIGHT
A Mother's Path to Self-Discovery

Chapter Thirteen
The Waning Crescent
Managing the Ebb and Flow

*We cannot be happy if we expect to live all the time at the
highest peak of intensity. Happiness is not a matter of intensity,
but of balance and order and rhythm and harmony.*
~ *Thomas Merton*

The Moon Sign in Astrology

As we discussed earlier in the chapter about moon sign astrology, the moon sign represents a person's emotions, instincts and the unconscious. It's an indicator of one's instinctive reactions – becoming the personality you keep hidden from others until you develop a comfort level with them.

The moon sign is a direct line to your inner being, allowing you to spontaneously feel and express joy as well as react to things that may cause you to feel discomfort or dissatisfaction. It's the part of you that enjoys the little sensualities of life and it's inextricably linked to the reactions you have to your environment.

Also in astrology, the meaning of the moon can be esoteric. It stands for infancy, childhood, your dreams, memory and your past – creating your inner psyche. A person's moon sign personality is often expressed in dreams – both daydreams and sleeping dreams.

Because the moon holds dominion over the emotional sphere, it can influence your receptivity to others and also how others feel about you. That's why a person's moon sign is especially important in love relationships. And for mothers, this love carries over to our children.

Scientists continue to study the moon's power over plant life, tides, emotions, fertility, menstruation and biorhythms. Astrologers continue to find new and subtle ways in which the moon influences our daily lives, particularly in the area of emotion.

Moonlight Musings

Review the meanings of your moon sign. How does it help you understand your emotional make-up? Considering all that you've been through in your life, does the description of your moon sign correlate with the emotional reactions you've had along the way?

Now imagine for a moment that you're the moon in the sky, looking down on the world through your emotional lens.

How do you see the world? How do you feel about the world? ~ Now zero in on your immediate environment. Through your moon sign lens, how do you emotionally connect with your current environment? Is there an emotional element missing?

If so, describe the missing element.

Take a few minutes to record these thoughts on this page.

The Waning Crescent

The waning crescent moon brings enlightenment at a deep level. It's a time of conscious growth, clarification of values and the surrender to a new future. Rebirth can occur during this phase and playfulness can come forth. This is when the moon diminishes from a sliver to the darkness of the new moon. It's a time of completion, inward-looking, and planning for the next phase in our lives.

This waning crescent moon is receptive and releasing. It's about letting go of the past and turning our thoughts and attention to the future. This phase involves a connection to the intellectual body, giving us a form of detachment – which will allow us to give an objective view toward the scenarios and the options in our lives. This moon phase magnifies our awareness of what was and what is to be.

The energy of the waning crescent phase is stimulated by hearing our own voice – both inner and outer. This voice carries the promise of our future. Liberation from the past must be attained in order to begin a path of consciousness and clarity. The function of this moon phase is to clear out old patterns in preparation for a new life cycle.

Withdrawal from the outside world may be necessary during this time. It's a time for dreaming and quiet contemplation. It's a time to be with ourselves and to listen to the voice within.

Moonlight Musings

As you retreat from the outside world and begin your quiet contemplation, take a deep breath and release it slowly. Do this several times until you begin to feel your body relax.

Now close your eyes and allow your inner wisdom to come forward. Ask yourself, what do I need to release? And what do I choose to take with me into the next phase of life?

Take a few minutes to ponder these questions and note your thoughts here.

Managing the Ebb and Flow

Humans aren't machines. We don't have a constant source of power from which we draw to perform complicated functions all the time, without breaks. Rather, our power supplies – or our energy and emotional levels – dip and rise with each hour of the day, and they even wax and wane on a much larger level. We find ourselves in periods of great motivation and energy – or periods where we just want to do what we need to do to survive and no more.

As mothers, we're accustomed to changing direction at any given moment. Many times we're okay with it – and just "go with the flow." But other times, we feel the resistance kicking in.

Alyssa, a mom with adult children, remembers when her second child went off to college. "I cried for a week. I realized that my babies were gone and I was alone. I had invested so much of my time and energy in raising them, that I felt completely frozen without them. My husband started worrying about me, so he arranged for a mini-vacation and we jetted off to a second honeymoon. And the time I spent with him took me back to a place where I was before kids. I started remembering the many things I wanted to do in my life, many of which I had not yet accomplished. It gave me the motivation to do those things. That trip really saved me."

When we refuse to listen to our cycles of high and low energy, we make things worse, not better. If our energy and emotional levels are off balance, we sometimes find ourselves falling off track with a strong need to stop and regroup. When this happens, we need to listen to our inner being – and go with the flow. If we feel a need to stop, we should stop. It may be the universe's way of telling us we need a breather.

When we give ourselves the gift of slowing down, it can be a really productive time. It can be good for the fermentation and incubation of ideas, and the processing and analysis of big decisions. It also provides the space for us to really resolve the missing pieces in our lives.

It is important to manage the ebb and flow of energy, emotion and motivation – on both a daily basis and a long-term basis. When you manage these cycles rather than ignore them, you are far more productive. But more importantly, you're happier.

In astrology, the moon rules our emotional being. And in science, the moon plays a key role in the ebb and flow of the ocean and the cycles of nature.

So how do our emotions affect the ebb and flow in our lives? And how can we manage the two so that they work together in a positive way?

As we go through the ebb and flow of life, it's important for us to reach a point of acceptance for "what is" – while holding on to our bigger vision. Once we connect with ourselves emotionally and understand how we may react to any given situation, we can respond accordingly.

Moonlight Musings

Imagine yourself taking an evening swim in the ocean. The light of the moon is reflecting on each wave as you float along with "what is." Relax and take in several deep breaths and ponder the ebb and flow of your life as it is right now.

As you think about the connections you've made with your inner being, how can you make an emotional connection with what is happening in your external world?

And how can you get to a place of acceptance with something you may or may not be able to control?

Take a few minutes to write about this in your journal.

Chapter Fourteen
The Blue Moon
Celebrating Your Uniqueness

*"Every once in a blue moon, something new comes along
that scrambles your preconceptions."*
~ *Anonymous*

The Blue Moon

The origin of the term "blue moon" is steeped in folklore, and its meaning has changed and acquired new nuances over time. Some folktales say that when there was a full blue moon, the moon had a face and talked to those in its light.

There are actual examples of the moon turning a blue color. When the Indonesian volcano Krakatoa exploded in 1883, its dust turned sunsets red and green, and gave the moon a blue tint that was seen around the world for almost two years. In 1927, a monsoon in India set up conditions for a blue moon. And the moon in Newfoundland, Canada turned blue in 1951 when huge forest fires in Alberta pushed smoke particles high into the sky blanketing its light.

There are probably at least six songs which use the term "blue moon" as a symbol of sadness and loneliness (which is the opposite twist on the Vedic meaning). In a number of these songs, the singer's moon turns to gold when he gets his love at the end of the lyrics.

According to the Farmer's Almanac, the definition of a blue moon is when a season has four full moons, instead of the usual three full moons. When this happens, the third full moon is considered the blue moon.

For those of us that follow the lunar calendar, a blue moon is a full moon that is not timed to the regular monthly pattern. Most years have twelve full moons – one per month.

But approximately every three years, there is an extra full moon. And when two full moons occur in a single month, the second full moon is called a "Blue Moon."

And we've all heard the saying, "once in a blue moon" – most commonly used to describe the rarity of an event or to refer to something that is considered "unusual" or "unique."

In this self-discovery process, the blue moon is intended to represent all that is unique about you. It's when your authenticity shines through loud and clear!

Embracing Your Authentic Self

When we accept our authentic self, the world just feels right. There are no worries about pleasing anybody but yourself. Living life authentically is the best gift we can give ourselves, our loved ones, and the world around us.

Nancy, a mother of four, found herself in a place of deep depression after the birth of her fourth child who was 10 years younger than her third. "I had spent so many years mothering my children that it dawned on me when we brought my youngest home, 'I won't have any time to call my own and pursue my dream of being a writer.' Luckily, I had a great partner who was fully supportive of my dream – and he helped me pull together what was needed to balance my career and motherhood."

When we are operating from a place of authenticity, we shine. Our smile becomes wider. Our eyes become brighter. Our hearts become bigger.

And everyone benefits – your family, your community, your country, your world. When we're at our best, magical things start to happen. Synchronicities start pouring in by the dozens. Doors of opportunity start to open.

It's the universe's way of saying, "You're on the right track!"

Moonlight Musings

Take a few minutes to list ten words that describe your authentic self. Put five words on one page – and five words on the next. And to make it a bit more fun, use different colored pens or markers.

Then draw or paste pictures that represent these words all over these pages.

And at the top of each page, write "I love my authentic self!"

Celebrating Your Uniqueness

Have you ever wondered if it's really true that no two snowflakes are alike? Scientists tell us that variations among complex snow crystals are purely limitless. Many snowflakes look alike – even under the microscope – but at closer examination, they differ. Even with millions and millions of snowflakes per year, the probability of two exactly identical snow crystals happening within the lifetime of the universe is practically zero.

Given the infinitely greater complexity of a human person, you can be absolutely sure that there never was, nor ever will be, anyone like you. This is the moment to ask yourself, "What is it that makes my own life unique?" You know the answer, but you need to express it to yourself simply and clearly. And within your answer, there lies your unique contribution to the unfolding of the universe. As Eckhart Tolle put it, "You are here to enable the divine purpose of the universe to unfold. That is how important you are!"

Is there a central preoccupation in your life, a melodic thread that runs through its entire symphony? If you can name it right now, you have much reason to be grateful. But even if you cannot name it, this guiding theme may be woven- somewhere – into the music of your days – and you need only listen more carefully.

As you become increasingly aware of your uniqueness, you will grow ever more grateful for the gift of being you and all you have to offer the world.

Moonlight Musings

Take the next 15 minutes to look at yourself in the mirror and pay close attention to everything you like about yourself. Look deep into your eyes and make a connection to everything that is great about you.

What is it that makes you unique? What is it that makes you like a snowflake?

Take time to write about the beauty of you – dancing in the moonlight under a star-filled sky, with an orchestra of crickets playing in the background.

And when you're finished, create a snowflake that represents your unique self. Decorate it in any way that feels authentic to you.

You can either paste it to the next page – or hang it in a special place.

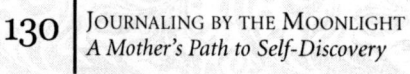

Chapter Fifteen
Dancing by the Moonlight

The more you praise and celebrate your life, the more there is in life to celebrate.
~ Oprah Winfrey

Creating a Circle of Celebration

As mothers, one of the things we have to work the hardest on is self-celebration – celebrating our gifts, our accomplishments, and our dreams. We're accustomed to supporting everyone else and celebrating their successes. Often times, we're the backbone of another's success.

It may be one of our children who are being recognized for making the school honor roll. We smile from ear to ear as we witness the award ceremony – never once thinking how hard we worked to make sure our children stayed on top of their school work.

It may be our husband who is honored for 25 years of service to his company. We stand proudly by his side as he receives a gift of recognition, never once thinking of the many nights we cared for the kids alone so he could take those extended business trips that were required in order to get the job done.

No matter what the celebration may be, it's a sure bet that we were a part of it in some way – big or small. As mothers, it's in our nature to nurture and support others.

But what's most overlooked is our personal success. Who is there to celebrate our success?

Terri describes the women in her book group as her lifelong friends. "I have known many of these women since our kids were babies. And here we are 20 years later. They have been with me through thick and thin, never once judging me. And they have celebrated my every success. I owe so much to these women. They have always given me the space to be who I am."

Moonlight Musings

Think about your circle of support. Who is there?

Go back to the tribe that you described in Chapter Nine and call them to the circle. It's time to celebrate your personal success.

Take some time to create your celebratory circle here. Begin by drawing a circle in your favorite color. Then place or draw an image that represents you and place it in the center of the circle. And around the inside of the circle, write the name of each member of your tribe. Feel free to fill up the circle with as many names as you need.

When you're done, add little bursts of color around the outside of the circle – to give the appearance of "sparkle" and "glow."

This is your time to shine – and to sparkle with celebration.

Making Yourself a Priority

When we contemplate our priorities, we often think about those related to our role as a mother. But in order to live more authentically, we should position our own personal priorities at the top of the list.

Our personal priorities are all the things you we would choose to do if we did not have so many responsibilities needing our constant attention. Personal priorities are those things we would do "if we only had the time, courage, money, talent, energy" – the list goes on and on.

Well now it's time to make YOU a priority! What is it that you enjoy doing most of all? What is it that brings you pure joy? What is it that exhilarates, enlivens and catalyzes you?

Don't think of anything that is prefaced by "I should do this" or "I ought to do this."

This is your time – your time to celebrate you!

Moonlight Musings

Picture yourself in a scenario that involves total pampering.

It may be a long bubble bath by candlelight or a day at the spa. It may be a day of scrapbooking with friends or an evening of reading your favorite book by the fireplace.

Think of an activity that you love to do – one that requires no attention to anyone but you.

Take a few minutes to describe this activity and how you feel when you think about it.

Celebrating Yourself

Self-celebration is the ability to honor yourself. It is the cornerstone to spontaneity and personal authenticity. It gives you permission to live your life joyfully.

When you're operating from a place of self-appreciation, everything else seems to fall into place around you. You begin to radiate happiness from your inner being.

Gratitude is truly the cornerstone of your personal success. When you are grateful for everything you are and for everything you bring to the world, magic begins to happen. Synchronicities begin to reveal themselves. And your life purpose becomes more and more clear.

Moonlight Musings

Now take a moment to thank your inner being for everything she has shown you throughout this process. If you have any questions for her, now is the time to ask. Write them on this page and give her some time to answer them. Leave plenty of room to record her answer. You may even want to use a different colored pen to record her wisdom.

And when you're finished, take another page to write a thank you letter to her, telling her what you've learned about yourself along the way. And tell her about your bigger vision and how it is her that will make it possible.

Make this letter as decorative as you can – as a special treat to her – and yourself.

When you're finished with the letter, go back to the place in this book where you wrote your dedication – and read what you wrote at the beginning of this process. Sit with this dedication for a few minutes – and then read the thank you letter you wrote a short while ago.

As you soak in these beautiful words, take a deep breath – breathing in the wisdom of your authentic self – and release your breath slowly – breathing out any anxieties, worries or old habits.

It's now time to move toward a life filled with authenticity and purpose – one step at a time.

Chapter Sixteen
Resources for the Journaling Mom

They didn't survive by eating each other; they survived by being resourceful.
~ Julie Schablitsky

To support you as you continue to live authentically, here is a list of some of my favorite resources (including my own individual and group coaching programs) and some of the books that I highly recommend as you continue on your journey of self-exploration.

Moonlight Moms Circle
www.MoonlightMomsCircle.com

Connect with a creative group of mothers who all value the importance of motherhood – and who desire to live a more spiritual, authentic and balanced life. Working more deeply with the phases of the moon as a source for spiritual transformation, mothers who are challenged by the loss of personal identity are gently guided on a path of self-discovery.

Using a variety of creative methods, including journaling and visual collage techniques, this coaching program allows for personal reflection with many opportunities to answer the question, "I'm a mother, but who am I really?" In a safe and nurturing environment, mothers will travel together on a spiritual, moonlit path toward a life of creative fulfillment.

Our Moonlight Moms Coaching Circles are based on the content of this book, "Journaling by the Moonlight: A Mother's Path to Self-Discovery" and its accompanying deck of journaling cards.

* * * * * * *

Journaling Moms Community
www.JournalingMoms.com

Here you'll find a nurturing group of mothers who all value the benefits of journal writing – and who desire to live a more authentic and balanced life, filled with purpose, passion and creative expression. Join us in our virtual Journaling Moms Cafe – or in our Journaling Mom Coaching Circles – where we'll explore new journal writing techniques with a variety of journaling prompts designed to guide you on a path of self-discovery. We'll also hear from many of the top experts in the field of personal writing as they lead us on a journey of self-exploration.

Once you join our Journaling Moms network, you'll be instantly connected to our virtual Journaling Moms Cafe where you'll find an array of interesting topics and resources, and many opportunities for conversation with other moms.

And for a more personal experience, our special six-month Journaling Mom Coaching Circles are designed for mothers who would like to explore deeper issues related to motherhood and self-care through the art of personal writing. Each month, moms will be gently guided on a journey that will focus on a particular area of motherhood. Topics in our coaching circles include: overwhelm and life balance, mother's guilt and resentment, the importance of self-care, building a strong support system, creating an authentic life, and living life with gratitude.

* * * * * * * *

Personal Writing Networks

Center for Journal Therapy
To make the healing art of journal writing accessible to all who desire self-directed change.
The Center for Journal Therapy lives this mission through its many outreach efforts. Books, speaking engagements, workshops, consultations, audiotapes and papers bring Kathleen Adams' wisdom to people and helping professionals everywhere. Popular media spreads the Center's core messages through coverage in newspapers and magazines. www.journaltherapy.com

International Association for Journal Writing
The International Association for Journal Writing (IAJW) will inspire and support your journal writing and keep you in the flow of your journaling cycle. This network is set up to help you write often, write in your own voice, and write more deeply. Featuring thirty of the most respected journal writing experts worldwide (including author Tina M. Games), the IAJW Journal Council offers a wide-ranging array of articles, teleseminars, videos, discussion forums, online groups and more! www.iajw.org

National Association of Memoir Writers
The National Association of Memoir Writers (NAMW) invites memoir writers from all over the world to connect, learn, and get inspired. The goal of the NAMW is to help memoir writers feel empowered with purpose and energy to begin and develop their life stories into a publishable memoir. The mission of the organization is to support memoir writers in their quest to write personal stories, leave a legacy, create a spiritual autobiography, and heal through writing. The NAMW helps connect, inspire, and support memoir writers from all over the world. www.namw.org

National Association of Women Writers
Where Women Unite to Write! ~ The National Association of Women Writers (NAWW) was founded in 2001 by fellow writer and entrepreneur, Sheri McConnell. With over 3000 members worldwide, the NAWW helps connect and educate their members on the world of writing through books, CDs, tele-events, physical chapter events and much more. You can subscribe to their free weekly newsletter by visiting their website. www.naww.org

Story Circle Network
The Story Circle Network is a national not-for-profit membership organization made up of women who want to document their lives and explore their personal stories through journaling, memoir, autobiography, personal essays, poetry, drama, and mixed-media. The faculty (which includes author Tina M. Games) leads online writing workshops designed for self-exploration. www.storycircle.org

* * * * * * *

Journaling Tools

LifeJournal Software
Here's the journal software program you've been searching for! This award-winning personal journal program is designed for you to write, reflect, and review securely and privately. Add depth and privacy to your journaling. LifeJournal is simple, yet sophisticated journal software, created by long-time diary writers. Sign up for a free demo at: www.lifejournal.com

Books on the Creative Process

The 12 Secrets of Highly Creative Women: A Portable Mentor
– *Gail McMeekin,* Conari Press, 2000.

The Power of Positive Choices: Adding and Subtracting Your Way to a Great Life
– *Gail McMeekin,* Conari Press, 2001.

Nine Modern Day Muses and a Bodyguard – *Jill Badonsky,* iUniverse, Inc., 2007.

The Artist's Way: A Spiritual Path to Higher Creativity
– *Julia Cameron,* Penguin Putnam, 2002.

A Vein of Gold: A Journey to Your Creative Heart – *Julia Cameron,* Penguin Putnam, 1996.

Your Heart's Desire: Instructions for Creating the Life You Really Want – *Sonia Choquette,* Three Rivers Press, 1997.

* * * * * * *

Books on the Journaling Process

A Forgiveness Journal: Letting Go of the Past – *Kristin E. Robertson,* Brio Leadership Press, 2009.

At a Journal Workshop – *Ira Progoff,* Penguin Putnam, 1992.

Journal to the Self: 22 Paths to Personal Growth – *Kathleen Adams,* Warner Books, 1990.

Life's Companion: Journal Writing as a Spiritual Quest – *Christina Baldwin,* Bantam Books, 1990.

Journaling for Joy – *Joyce Chapman,* Newcastle Publishing Company, 1995.

Journalution: Journaling to Awaken Your Inner Voice, Heal Your Life, and Manifest Your Dreams – *Sandy Grayson,* New World Library, 2005.

The Power of Memoir: How to Write Your Healing Story – *Linda Joy Myers, Ph.D.,*
Jossey-Bass, 2010.

The Way of the Journal: A Journal Therapy Workbook – *Kathleen Adams,*
Sidran Press, 1998.

The Write Way to Wellness – *Kathleen Adams,* Center for Journal Therapy, 2000.

Writing as a Way of Healing: How Telling Our Stories Transforms Our Lives
– *Louise DeSalvo,* Beacon Press, 1999.

Writing to Save Your Life: How to Honor Your Story Through Journaling
– *Michele Weldon,* Hazelden, 2001.

* * * * * * *

Books on the Spiritual Journey

A Weekend to Change Your Life – *Joan Anderson,* Broadway Books, 2006.

Calling the Circle: The First and Future Culture – *Christina Baldwin,* Bantam Books, 1994.

Callings: Finding and Following an Authentic Life – *Gregg Levoy,* Three Rivers Press, 1997.

Compass of the Soul: 52 Ways Intuition Can Guide You to the Life of Your Dreams
– *Lynn Robinson,* Broadway Books, 2006.

Everyday Grace: Having Hope, Finding Forgiveness, and Making Miracles
– *Marianne Williamson,* Penguin Putnam, 2002.

Finding Your Own North Star: Claiming the Life You Were Meant to Live
– *Martha Beck,* Three Rivers Press, 2001.

I Will Not Die An Unlived Life: Reclaiming Purpose and Passion
– *Dawna Markova,* Conari Press, 2000.

Live Your Dream: Discover and Achieve Your Life Purpose
– *Joyce Chapman,* New Page Books, 2002.

About the Author
Tina M. Games

Tina is a certified creativity and life purpose coach, working with mothers who are challenged by issues related to the loss of personal identity and who desire a more authentic life – filled with purpose, passion and creative expression. Her book, *Journaling by the Moonlight: A Mother's Path to Self-Discovery* and the accompanying deck of journaling cards (by the same name) are based on her signature coaching program designed around the phases of the moon. She leads "Moonlight Muse" retreats twice a year (around the full moon) for women who want to reconnect with their authentic self.

Also certified as a journaling workshop facilitator, Tina leads virtual and in-person workshops, and coaching circles for mothers who want to explore their passion for journal writing, while expanding their personal support systems. She works both privately and in group settings – and facilitates her own online network, the "Journaling Moms Café."

Tina serves on the Journal Council for the International Association for Journal Writing where she is joined by 30 other journaling experts worldwide. They offer a variety of articles, resources, webinars, and teleclasses on journal writing to association members.

In addition to her work as a personal coach and workshop facilitator, Tina volunteers her time as an advocate on issues of importance to mothers on a local, state and national level. She is also a frequent guest on blog talk radio shows – and speaks to groups and organizations on the importance of creating support systems and how to journal your way to a more authentic life.

Tina lives in Alexandria, Virginia with her husband and their two children, Spencer and Holly.

To learn more about Tina and her work, please visit her websites at www.MoonlightMomsCircle.com and www.JournalingMoms.com.